COCONUT AND ECONOMIC DEVELOPMENT

COCONUT AND ECONOMIC DEVELOPMENT

S.N. Yogish
Lecturer, Dos In Economics
Jnana Sahyadri, Kuvempu University
Shankarghatta-577451

SERIALS PUBLICATIONS
New Delhi

First Published – 2004

ISBN : 81-86771-51-4

Published by

Head Office : SERIALS PUBLICATIONS
4, B.S.S. Hall, Khyber Pass Market,
Civil Lines, Delhi-110054 (India)
Fax: 91-11-23812678
Phone : 23245225
e-mail : serials@satyam.net.in

Branch Office : *4830/24, Prahlad Stret, Ansari Road, Darya Ganj, New Delhi-110002 (India)*

PREFACE

Coconut is the most important palm in the world but remains predominantly a small holder's crop from time immemorial. Millions of people in the tropical regions depend on the coconut palm for their livelihood.

The Coconut Development Board has launched a massive new planting programme for coconut in the country. The programme provides assistance to the growers in the form of new planting subsidy for bringing additional area under coconut. As a result coconut culture is fast spreading not only in the traditional coconut growing states but in other states also where ecological features were not considered congenial for coconut culture till recently.

In the special drive initiated by the Coconut Development Board for the expansion of coconut culture thousands of small farmers spread over the different states are involved.

The usual extension support in the field, it is also essential to extend adequate technical guidance to them in the form of popular publications on improved coconut culture.

Coconut palms may be made to produce satisfactory yields by adopting proper management practices, particularly recommended dose of fertilizers twice in a year, providing summer irrigation, adopting multi-storeyed cropping and mixed farming systems.

This book "Coconut and Economic Development" presents a comprehensive information on the coconut palm and its products will be useful to planters, researchers and extension workers and also general readers. It covers all aspects of coconut cultivation including, Trends in area production and productivity, Cost of cultivation, Production of coconut, Marketing of coconut.

This book is the result of my research work carried at the Department of Economics, Karnatak University, Dharwad. I am deeply indebted to my Guide,

Dr. S.R. Narappanavar, M.Sc., M.A., Ph.D., Professor and Head, Department of Studies in Economics, Karnatak University, Dharwad, for his sympathetic and competent guidance and valuable suggestions at each and every stage of this work. In spite of his heavy schedule, he was very kind to go through the chapters of the thesis and made corrections and suggested many improvements.

I am grateful to the Librarians of Karnatak University and University of Agricultural Sciences, Dharwad, Institute for Social and Economic Change, Bangalore, Central Plantation Crops Research Institute, Kasargod, Kuvempu University, Shankaraghatta, for having patiently providing me whatever I wanted to consult the Documents, Books and Journals.

I am specially indebted to my wife Smt. Mamatha, who assisted me in tabulating the data and encouraged me to complete the thesis at an early date. She has been an unfailing source of inspiration at every stage of my research work.

I thank my publisher Mr. Vijay Kumar, New Delhi, who has taken keen interest to bring out this book in a short time.

S.N. YOGISH

CONTENTS

Preface v

List of Tables & Maps ix

1. Introduction 1

2. Methodology, Database and Profile of Study Area 21

3. Trends in Area, Production and Productivity of Coconut 41

4. Cost of Cultivation 69

5. Production of Coconut 103

6. Marketing of Coconut 117

7. Summary and Conclusions 139

Bibliography 153

LIST OF TABLES & MAPS

TABLES

2.1 Taluka-wise Area of Tumkur District 30
2.2 Net Sown Area in Different Talukas of Tumkur District, 1994-95 31
2.3 Distribution of Land-Holdings During the Year 1994-95 32
2.4 Area Under Major Crops in Tumkur District During 1994-95 33
2.5 Taluka-wise Distribution of Area Under Coconut in Tumkur District 1995-96 35
2.6 Different Sources of Irrigation During 1994-95 36
3.1 Area, Production and Productivity of Coconut in Different Countries 42
3.2 Statewise Area and Production of Coconut in India,1991-92 44
3.3 Size of Coconut Holdings in Major Producing States 44
3.4 Area Under Coconut in Major Coconut Growing States in India 46
3.5 Production of Coconut in Major Coconut Growing States in India 47
3.6 Productivity Per Hectare in Major Coconut Growing States in India 49
3.7 Area, Production and Productivity of Coconut in Karnataka 52
3.8 Area, Production and Productivity of Coconut in Tumkur District 53
3.9 Area Under Coconut in Major Coconut Growing Districts in Karnataka 54
3.10 Production of Coconut in Major Coconut Growing Districts in Karnataka 55
3.11 Productivity of Coconut in Major Coconut Growing Districts in Karnataka 55
3.12 Trends in Area, Production and Productivity (Yield) at National, State and District Levels 57
3.13 Outlay for the Coconut Development Board Programmes for the VIII Plan Period (1992-97) 66

3.14 Allocations for Coconut Development Under Different Plans 66
4.1 Distribution of Farmers According to Family Size 69
4.2 Distribution of Sample Farmers According to Education 70
4.3 Area Under Coconut and Other Crops Grown by the Sample Farmers 71
4.4 Per Acre Cost of Cultivation of Coconut in Case of Small Farmers (Irrigated) 72
4.5 Per Acre Cost of Cultivation of Coconut in Case of Medium Farmers (Irrigated) 80
4.6 Per Acre Cost of Cultivation of Coconut in Case of Large Farmers (Irrigated) 87
4.7 Per Acre Cost of Cultivation of Coconut in Case of Small Farmers (Unirrigated) 92
4.8 Per Acre Cost of Cultivation of Coconut in Case of Medium Farmers (Unirrigated) 96
4.9 Per Acre Cost of Cultivation of Coconut in Case of Large Farmers (Unirrigated) 100
5.1 Area, Production and Productivity of the Sample Farmers 1994-95 105
5.2 Production of Tender, Desiccated Coconut and Copra by Different Size Group of Farmers, 1994-95 109
5.3 Production Per Acre of Tender, Desiccated Coconut and Copra by Different Size Group of Sample Farmers 113
6.1 Sales and Prices of Copra in Ulliyar APMC Yard, 1984-1996 120
6.2 Sales and Prices of Desiccated Coconut in Ulliyar APMC Yard, 1984-1996 121
6.3 Sales and Prices of Copra in Tiptur APMC Yard, 1982-1984 122
6.4 Sales and Prices of Desiccated Coconut in Tiptur APMC Yard, 1982-1994 123
6.5 Sales of Tender, Desiccated Coconut and Copra by the Sample Farmers, 1994-1995 124
6.6 Sales of Tender Coconut According to Farm Size in the Sample Area, 1994-1995 126
6.7 Sales of Desiccated Coconut According to Farm Size in the Sample Area, 1994-1995 127
6.8 Sales of Copra According to Farm Size in the Sample Area, 1994-1995 128
6.9 Sales of Tender, Desiccated Coconut and Copra Per Acre According to Farm Size 1994-1995 (Irrigated Farms) 130

6.10 Sales of Tender, Desiccated Coconut and Copra Per Acre According to Farm Size 1994-1995 (Unirrigated) 132
6.11 Income from By-Products of Coconut Per Acre According to Farm Size, 1994-1995 134
6.12 Cost, Gross Returns, Net Profit and Output-Input Ratio in Coconut Cultivation by the Sample Farms 136

MAPS

1. Karnataka State - Tumkur District 22
2. Tumkur District - Taluka Headquarters - Sample Villages 23

CHAPTER 1

INTRODUCTION

The coconut palm is one of the most useful and important trees in the world and it has a long association with human history of over thousand years. Since then, this crop has been considered both as an object of reverence in the local tradition and as the most profitable economic enterprise/ activity[1].

The coconut palm, cocos nucifera Linn., with its tall, slender and uniformly thick stem and massive crown with large number of leaves, bearing bunches of nuts in their axiles is one of the beautiful and useful trees in the world. It perhaps yields more products of use to mankind than any other tree. It is no wonder that the palm is looked upon with reverence and affection by the inhabitants of the coconut producing countries and considered as Kalpa Vruksha[2].

Each and every part of the coconut palm is useful in one way or another. The tender coconut supplies a very popular, refreshing and satisfying beverage. The raw kernel is an important article of food. The oil from the nut is used in cooking and in the manufacture of soap and other toilet requisites. The coconut oil cake is a valuable cattle feed. Fibre from the husk is used in the manufacture of coir ropes, mats and mattings. The trunk otherwise called 'porcupine wood', is used in house construction and furniture making. The leaves after plaiting are used to thatch houses. The juice obtained on tapping the inflorescence is rich in sugar and is converted into jaggery, sugar, vinegar and sweet or fermented toddy. The products of commercial importance are copra, oil, oil-cake, desiccated coconut and fibre[3].

"The importance of the palm lies in the fact that not only does it supply food, drink and shelter but also provides raw material for a number of important industries. It is also essentially a crop of the small land holder who obtains cash for the purchase of necessities of life by the sale of coconut and coconut products. In the Philippines, 82 percent of the total area under coconut is composed of small holdings with an average of about two hectares. In India the average is estimated to be less than an acre. In Ceylon, small holdings of less than 20 acres each coconut for over 80 percent of the area under the crop. In Malaya, out of total area of 6.0 lakh of acres 3.9 lakh/ acres are composed of holdings of less than 100 acres of extent.[4]"

The coconut industry is intimately connected with the economic and domestic life of the inhabitants of the coconut growing countries. It provides employment and perhaps the only source of livelihood to many thousands of people. Thus in Philippines eight million people or more than a third of the entire population is dependent upon this industry for the livelihood. In India, according to Gopalan5, the coconut industry gives full or part time employment the total population of Kerala comprising the districts of Trivendrum, Quilon, Kottayam, Trichur, Kozhikode, Cannanore and Palghat. In Ceylon, the coconut industry is the main source of livelihood and provides employment for nearly 3 million of its population.

Coconut serves as one of the important sources of food. In India, coconut is consumed in the form of tender nuts, raw kernel, copra, coconut oil and desiccated coconut. According to Gopalan6, the nut equivalent of coconuts and coconut products consumed in India comes to 2893 million or about 84 percent of the total production in the country. In Ceylon, the per capita consumption of coconuts is estimated at 140 nuts per annum which amounts to annual consumption of 1000 million nuts out of an estimated production of 2000 million. In Philippines 4 to 5 percent of the production is reported to be consumed locally.

Besides, more coconut plantations are needed to meet the growing demands viz., food, oil, coir, medicine etc., and has great economic importance. In addition to this, it is also evident that there is enormous potentiality for expanding coconut plantation/ crops in Karnataka. Hence the study about coconut cultivation has gained much importance[7].

Consequently, in most of agriculturally dominant countries, the economies of coconut cultivation has become a subject of great importance. The countries like Bangla Desh, Philippines, Indonesia, Sri Lanka and India have raised many questions regarding coconut cultivation/ crops. Particularly, coconut crop cultivation has attracted the attention of Indian agriculture since modernisation. Also India being the third largest production of nuts in the world, and particularly, in India. Karnataka State stands third in the production of nuts, understanding the economies of the coconut plantation assumes paramount importance. Moreover the cultivation of coconut crop is most suitable for Indian land holdings (of small size) providing large employment[8].

Coconut tree yields more products of use to mankind than any other tree known to man. The variety of products derived from the coconut palms throughout the world is practically boundless. The nuts of the coconut palm could truly be counted among the most important fruits of the world. The tender nut supplies a refreshing beverage and the raw kernel is an important article of food in all coconut growing countries[9]. A number of commodities are derived from the nut which enter international commodity markets.

The dried kernel-copra, is a major source of oil. Coconut oil is an important and one of the oldest items used in the manufacture of soaps, other cosmetics and in margarine. Poonac or "pressed cake" which is the meal after oil extraction is a valuable livestock feed. Desiccated coconut is used widely in bakery and confectionary trades the world ovcr.

The husk of the nuts provides a high quality hand fibre which is used in numerous industries. Locally, fibre provides the valuable raw material in spinning coir yarn and in the manufacture of coir ropes, cordage, brooms, woven carpets and many other utility items.

The hard shell is mainly used locally as a fuel but there is a heavy demand for carbonized coconut shells in overseas markets. Some of this shell-charcoal is converted into activated charcoal which has important industrial uses as a combating air and water pollution[10].

India is the third largest coconut producing country in

the world. The Philippines and Indonesia occupy the first and second place respectively. In India, coconut culture occupies about 1.2 million hectares spread over the entire coastal belt. Some interior places which are otherwise suitable are also utilised for coconut culture. Such places could be seen in parts of Karnataka. Bihar and Madhya Pradesh. Among the major coconut growing states, Kerala ranks first where 57.74 percent of the total coconut hectarage and 49.28 percent of the total production in the country are concentrated. While this is so, the unit productivity of the crop in the Kerala State is low compared to that of other states. The productivity of the crop in Kerala is as low as 4925 nuts per hectare, whereas it is 10651 nuts in Tamil Nadu and 5215 nuts in Karnataka[11]. Thus the productivity in Tamil Nadu and Karnataka is higher than that in Kerala.

REVIEW OF STUDIES

A general survey of the studies conducted earlier covering several aspects with a view to understanding the functioning of the economic of cost, production and marketing of various agricultural commodities is attempted here. The studies on all major agricultural commodities in India have been covered chronologically categorywise. The time horizon is from 1969 to 1996.

CEREALS

A study[12] on "cost of production of wheat in Punjab during the 1973-74 season reveals that the cost of production per quintal of wheat in Punjab increased from Rs. 67.10 in 1972-73 to Rs. 74.34 in 1973-74. This was due to the rise in cost of cultivation per hectare from Rs. 1650.54 in 1972-73 to Rs. 2037.14 in 1973-74. This rise in the cost of cultivation per hectare was proportionately much more than an increase in yield per hectare. The rise in yield per hectare was primarily due to the increased use of most of the inputs, which together with the rise in input prices, also explained the increase in the total cost of cultivation per hectare. As a result of the increase in both the yields per hectare and the average post-harvest prices of the grain and the by-product, the gross income per hectare of wheat increased during the year under review. Since the increase in the total cost of cultivation per hectare was much less than that in gross income, net income per hectare over total cost of cultivation rose manifold between 1972-73 and 1973-74. Net income over cash and kind expenses nearly doubled between the two years.

Subba Rao[13] has assessed the economic efficiency of rice marketing system and evaluated the impact of public intervention on the marketing system with special reference to the West Godavari districts of Andhra Pradesh during 1968-72. The author has fallowed twin approaches i.e., concurrent marketing margin and structure - conduct - performance for the assessment of economic efficiency in the marketing of rice at the village and institutional levels. The cross section analysis has revealed that large farmers realized higher prices than small farmers although considerable variation existed between prices received by the sample farmers. Further, the losses suffered by the small farmers due to various imperfections in the marketing system do not appear to be as large as is generally believed.

A study by Ratna-Reddy[14] on size productivity relationship between farm size and productivity holds good in majority of the regions. It was mainly due to the higher labour intensity on small farms and also due to intensity of material inputs, to some extent. Higher labour intensity on small farms was due to the availability of cheap family labour and also the use of more hired labour.

As far as net returns to farming was concerned, the small farmers were not able to convert their output advantages to higher net profits due to their higher total expenditure especially in the case of local paddy. This was due to the reason that small farmers try to maximize their output while large farmers try to maximize profits. The reasons for this may be (i) Small farmers produce more in order to meet the higher food requirements of a large family, (ii) and they may not be able to reduce their total expenditure by adopting labour substituting techniques like tractors as they cannot afford.

PULSES

Rahman and Kashem[15] studied growing and marketing problems of pulse crops in Bangla Desh High price of fertilizer, high cost of production, lack of capital, disease problem and high cost of pesticides, high price of seeds and high irrigation cost were found to be the major factors in growing pulse crops. Reduction of price of improved seeds of pulse crops, distribution of credit, reduction of prices of fertilizer and pesticides, provision of irrigation and drainage facilities were the important measures suggested to overcome the various problems of cultivation of pulses. Provision of improved storage facilities, providing price protection to farmers from middlemen were the measures suggested to overcome the marketing problems of pulses.

PLANTATION CROPS

P.P.Madappa[16] conducted a study of cost of production of coffee in India. Coffee as a plantation and foreign exchange earning crop is well-known in India. The need for and the importance of the study of cost of production of coffee can not be overemphasized. Several cost studies on coffee have been made in India. But these studies are subjected to several limitations. This study attempted to overcome some of the limitations and to fill the gaps. The objectives of the study were (i) to review the studies on cost of production of coffee in India; (ii) to study the cost of production of coffee by survey method, covering estates of almost all size-groups.

The cost of new planting as available form the Report of the Plantation Inquiry Commission (1956), varied from about Rs.1,000 to 2,000 per acre for the first year. In yet another recent study it varied from Rs. 2,500 per acre in 1965-66 to Rs. 3,000 in 1969-70. The estimated replanting cost as shown in the study was Rs. 2,000 per acre for the first five years in 1965-66 and Rs. 2,500 in 1969-70.

As per the studies available, the cost of production of matured/ bearing plants per acre varied anything between Rs. 400 and Rs, 700 in 1953. In 1958 the estimated cost of production was Rs. 836 per acre. The estimated cost of production in 1961 was Rs. 1,300 per acre. The main findings of this study are : (a) The average coffee area per planter was about 55 acres, with a range from 10 acres to above 200 acres. The average paddy growing area per planter was about 3 acres, and coffee and orange growing area was about 15 acres. (b) Estates of smaller size contained more younger plants than the estates of bigger size (c) On an average, the net expenditure per acre of paddy was about Rs. 235 and for orange Rs. 150. The average net income per acre from paddy was about Rs. 90 and from orange about Rs. 90 (d) The total cost of production of coffee per acre was about Rs.900. Out of the total cost of production, cultivation cost accounted for about Rs. 500 (55 per cent), cost of preparing the produce for the market for about Rs. 100 (9 per cent) and 'other costs' for about Rs. 300 (30 per cent). Inputwise, labour cost accounted for about 40 per cent of the total cost and material cost for about 20 per cent. (e) The average pre-tax profit per acre of coffee production was Rs. 275. However, the estates under the size-group of 100 to 200 acres incurred a loss of Rs. 11 per acre. On the basis of output-input co-efficients under the different size-groups of estates, it appeared as though it was more economical to own an estate of the size of either 200 acres and above, between 50 and 100 acres or between 10 and 25 acres than to own an estate of the size of 100 to 200 acres or 25 to 50 acres.

COCONUT

There are several studies, covering one aspect or the other, on cost of cultivation, production and marketing of coconut conducted by many researchers. A brief review has been done here.

P.K.Das[17] studied the estimation of production cost and returns for coconut in Kerala. This study reveals that coconut cultivation under good management is profitable in Kerala. Since the scope of this paper was limited to monoculture of west coast tall variety of coconut, the full economic potential of this crop with hybrids as well as under inter/ mixed cropping has not been expressed here. As it appears, owing to the economic pressure on land for deriving maximum benefits from the available resources, most of the coconut gardens in Kerala are now intercropped with annuals, semi-perennials and perennial crops. Under these situations, the cost of production of nuts found to be lower and the returns from the coconut- based farming systems are higher than what has been observed in this study.

C. Latha Bastime and M.P. Abdurazak[18] studied cost and

returns from coconut holdings of different sizes in northern Kerala. The study revealed that the cost of maintenance per hectare was Rs. 6297.65, Rs. 5431.62, Rs. 5100.52 and Rs. 4183.73 respectively for the four categories of farms. The average cost was worked out to Rs. 4442.05 per hectare. Sixty five percent of the total cost was incurred for application of manures and fertilizers. Inputwise analysis showed that 45.19 percent of the total cost was incurred on manures and 41.16 percent on labour. Only very limited expenditure was made on plant protection chemicals. The family labour utilization showed wide variation i.e., 34.73 percent in stratum I to 6.59 percent in stratum III. The average net profit per hectare was worked out Rs. 10360.43.

N. Nagaraj, K.N.R. Sastry and M.G. Chandrakanth[19] studied economic considerations in selecting coconut enterprise. The performance of garden provides ample security for the funds lent since the farmers continue to get substantial returns over costs for sufficiently a long period. The various measures like Internal Rate of Return, Benefit Cost Ratio, Net Present Value and Pay Back Period provide ample proof in this regard. Therefore lending for coconut orchard and also establishment of the same for earning income need not be considered as a risky proposition. Further this situation becomes more favourable if it is complemented with other crops and livestock enterprises. In actual experience also, here are evidences where the farmers having coconut gardens, have successfully utilised space, water and sunshine for growing mulberry and coca.

V.M. Jakhade and V.P. Kurian[20] conducted a study in two districts of Kerala state with an objective to find out the amount of expenditure incurred on fertilizers and manures and its proportion to total expenditure on coconut cultivation and to assess the amount of credit required for the purpose by different classes of coconut growers. In the light of above objectives the study indicated that cultivators had grown more than one crop like paddy, arecanut, topico, plantation etc. And with regards to expenditure, it showed that there was variance between the regions and the expenditure on fertilizers and manures accounted for more than 70 percent to total expenditure. Besides the analysis indicated that the loans/ credit issued for coconut cultivation amounted to only 20 percent of the total credit/ loan.

Chandan Mukherjee (1975)[21] in his study estimated cost of maintenance of coconut plantation at 1973-74 prices before the doubling of fertilizer prices. The cost of maintenance was found to be Rs. 10.50 per nut bearing tree per year. According to the study the cost of maintenance and procurement during the first four years will be less than that during the fifth year onwards.

H.M.G. Herath[22] studied the performance of replanting of senile holdings in the coconut sector in Sri Lanka. The study indicates that subsidies have not been effective. Many farmers do not undertake replanting due to deferment of present incomes. Studies have been made to evaluate the various ways by which replanting could be made attractive. One approach that holds promise is the interplanting of coconut land with banana plantation and subsequent replacement with coca when the banana phases out. This system gives incomes from the second year onwards and hence mitigates the severity of loss of income in the early years of replanting. Both the economic and financial rates of return from this area were attractive. The economic benefit-cost ratios were higher than the financial benefit-cost ratios. Sensitive analysis shows the financial and economic returns were still high even under unfavourable assumptions.

Study made by H.I. Dalvi[23] and others on the cost of marketing margins has shown that marketing of coconut in Sindhudurg district in Maharashtra is simple and not involving many intermediaries as the demand was restricted to the district only. Most of the produce was consumed locally and hence nuts were sold by local producers to consumers. Direct selling to the consumers was found to be the most profitable one than selling through the wholesalers. The farmers got maximum share in consumers rupee, while in case of latter it was minimum. Co-operatives must therefore be encouraged to come forward in the marketing of coconuts as this channel offers better share to the producers in the consumers price.

Mathew[24] observes on the need for irrigating coconut palms that "palms undoubtedly benefit from irrigation and this can be done on a small scale when it is possible to divert streams or to store water in small tanks, as in South

India. But it is unlikely that large areas of palms will continue to be cultivated in areas where rainfall is low and badly distributed and little attention is currently being paid to the possibilities of irrigation of coconut palms, except in general terms and as applicable to smallholdings."

C.K.B. Nambiar and others[25] conducted a study on application of organic manure to reduce coconut mortality on coastal sand. Field experiment was carried out to assess the role of different organic sources along with normal application in the establishment of coconut on literal sand. The application of cattle manure, coirdust, coconut shading, forest leaves, along with NPK resulted in a remarkable reduction in mortality. These applications increased the growth characteristics like palm height and number of leaves etc.

Viswanathan Pillai's[26] study on coconut palms in 1975 indicates that every part of the tree has important economic uses. The chief product is the coconut kernel which is converted into copra from which coconut oil is extracted. Coconut kernel and oil are important food items especially for the people of Kerala. Coconut husk is used for the extraction of the strongest and most enduring natural fibre which is the raw material for the coir industry. Coconut shell, besides being an efficient fuel, is put to industrial use in making activated charcoal. It is also used for several handicraft products.

India accounted for about 1/5th of the worlds output of coconuts in the year 1975. Among Indian States, Kerala occupies a unique position in the matter of coconut production. The state accounted for more than 70 percent of the all India area under coconut and was responsible for 2/3rds of the total output of the crop in the year 1975.

The trend in production over the last decades (1970) was not quite encouraging. Two factors have been mentioned for the low rate of increase in production. The first and more apparent one is damage being done to the crops by the root and bud diseases which affected a considerable part of the coconut tracts of the State. Second one is unfavourable conditions of monsoon.

Experiments conducted by N.Krishnaji and others[27] at

the Central Planation Crops Research Institute showed that it is possible to raise the yield of garden land through the introduction of mixed and inter-cropping. A hectare of land under coconut cultivation could generate a net income of the order of Rs. 5,000 in the year 1976, even on plantation where the 2/3rds of the total nut bearing trees provided optimal farming practices. The implications of these experiments vary from region to region within Kerala.

According to Kunikrishnan[28], coconut plant offers more than any other plantation crop in the tropics. It has also been called as the Kalpa Vruksha or the "all giving tree". Besides, coconut trees give continuous yield after 6 or 7 years of planting and accommodate variety of other crops along with it. Coconut also has commercial product like coconut oil, coir etc. Thus coconut crop is a source of income, consumer goods, and industrial promotion and has been an object of reverence in local tradition.

Gita Aravamutham[29] analyses the position of coconut crop in Kerala and states the various reasons for poor productivity. The low yield per tree and low quality of the nut is due to over crowding of trees, lack of irrigation and manuring. And also held opinion that Kerala is relatively well versed in commercial utilization of the coconut and there is a need for revamping production and redistribution of coconut.

Jamool Unni[30] studied the changes in the cropping pattern in Kerala and found out some evidences on substitution of coconut for rice. As this paper examines shifts in cropping pattern in Kerala in the part two decades, it appears that garden-land crops (particularly coconut) have been gaining at the expense of wet-land crops (particularly paddy), It is also observed that the major part of the increase in area took place in most districts between 1960-61 and 1968-69. The percentage increase in the area under coconut was 37 percent- much larger than increase in the area under rice (12.2 percent) during this period.

T.C. Mohan's[31] study in 1988 points out that Kerala is well known for its coconut production and its productivity from 1956-57 to 1985-86, it has been accounting for 60-65 percent of all India production. The main issue discussed was that why despite favourable agroclimatic condition there is a declining trend in area, yield and production of coconuts in Kerala. The available findings from various studies neither have provided sufficient explanations nor tackled the problems of coconut economy. To bridge the gap and to increase production and productivity, the State Government was asked to take up comprehensive policy measures like subsidy incentives, providing quality seedlings and extension activities.

Narayana and others[32] conducted a survey on coconut development in Kerala State with special reference to Ernakulum district. They found that the area under coconut cultivation has been showing a declining trend, and coconut production also has shown a declining trend. The small increase in production of coconut is not sufficient for percapita consumption of nuts because of growth in population. The fluctuation of prices of coconut and coconut oil has been another area of study in the book.

M.V. George and P.T. Joseph[33] studied the nature of fluctuations in the prices of coconuts and suggested a scheme for stabilization of coconut prices in Kerala. The study was undertaken to examine the long-term trend as well as the annual fluctuations in prices with a view to stabilize the price and income of the growers. Since stability in prices is important for consumers as coconut products constitute a major item of consumption to the poorer section of the State population. The study held that, in spite of the large increase in the area under coconut (about 44%) during 70-71, the increase in the production has been very less (24%). It is also said that the fall in the production was due to heavy incidence of diseases.

P.K. Thampan[34] studied promoting product diversification and by-product utilization in coconut industry in India. Copra making and oil milling are the only coconut based processing activities which have developed on an organized scale. Consequently the economic prosperity of both the farmers and the processers at the primary level is closely woven around the fortunates of milling industry. Of late, the dependence of coconut industry on a single commodity, (coconut oil) has been causing significant instability to the coconut based economy of many states. This situation has to be changed by promoting diversified uses of all the major coconut products and the application of viable technologies for the economic utilization of valuable by-products of coconut. For achieving this objective adequate priority has to be given for technological research besides creating facilities for technology transfer, entrepreneurial development and techno-economic feasibility, including pilot-testing. Progress in this direction could eventually develop a vibrant processing sector when it would become possible to facilitate the economic utilization of all the products and by-products of coconut.

P.Raveendra[35] analyses Demand, Consumption pattern and consumer acceptability of desiccated coconut in India. According to him there is a good scope for increasing the consumption of desiccated coconut in the households especially in the north Indian Centres. The product should be made available in small packages of 200 or 500 gm in the provision stores where the regular household items are sold. There is general acceptability on colour and taste of the product. The need is to educate the general public about the advantages of using desiccated coconut. This can be done by different methods such as advertisement through various media, demonstrations distribution of sample packets at concessional rates etc. Even in Kerala where fresh coconut is a regular article for food preparations, there is scope for improving the consumption because of the convenience and time saving factors. With proper distribution of the product along with necessary propaganda, the consumption of desiccated coconut in the households could be stepped up substantially.

C. Narasimhappa[36] observes that coconut is one of the most valuable and essential commodities in India. According to him its marketing has been jeopardized by many inherent reasons and faulty policies of Government which can very well be corrected in order to brighten the prospects of coconut and its products in Indian markets. The efforts are also needed to revamp the present marketing system in favour of grower-consumer linked system, in which the growers and consumers are the participants, and exploitation will no longer be a part of the marketing system. By involving growers in processing- marketing activities, the much desired vertical integration could be achieved.

N.S.P.Rebello, P.G.Chengappa and Lalith Achota[37] in 1987 attempted to estimate the cyclical patterns in arrivals and prices of coconuts in four important regulated markets of Karnataka. The price series in all the markets were dominated by the trend variable caused by the high prices prevailing during the years 1983-85. The trends in prices were reflected by a trend in arrivals as well, which is indicative of the long run supply adjustment to price. The arrivals were characterized by long and 31/2 years in Bangalore. By and large the amplitudes of the price cycles indicated a degree of instability in the price. However, it is observed that these cycles in quantitites did not have price dependence.

NEED FOR THE STUDY

From the foregoing review of literature it can be inferred that very few empirical works have be done on coconut plantation with particular reference to Karnataka. An in-depth study covering different aspects of coconut plantation such as cost of cultivation, production, yield, and marketing of coconut etc., if an urgent need of the coconut economy. Therefore, a study has been undertaken to know various aspects of coconut cultivation and to provide vital information about the prospect of coconut cultivation in Tumkur district as well as in Karnataka.

OBJECTIVES

The primary objectives of the study are to go into the crux of the problems of cost of production, yield and marketing of coconut in Karnataka. However, the specific objectives have been crystallized as follows:

(i) To estimate the trends in the area, production and productivity of coconut crop in Tumkur District and also in Karnataka.

(ii) To estimate the average cost of cultivation of coconut, production, productivity, income received and output-input ratio in the cultivation of coconut plantation in Tumkur District.

(iii) To study the economic viability of raising coconut plantation in Tumkur District.

HYPOTHESES

The following hypotheses are framed and tested in the study:

(i) Area, production and productivity of coconut plantation have increased significantly in Tumkur District and also in Karnataka.

(ii) Coconut plantation is profitable in the Tumkur District.

(iii) Big farmers are benefited more by coconut plantation as compared to small and medium farmers.

LIMITATIONS

The present study is beset with certain obvious limitations. They are enumerated here.

(i) Only four villages were selected for the study. Hence, results are largely applicable to those areas where similar conditions prevail.

(ii) The interview method of data collection requires the respondents to recall from their memory about previous agricultural operations and crop results. Hence, the findings may be subjected to errors.

(iii) Not much research work has been carried out and published on the economics of coconut farming in Karnataka. Hence, the study has been done on the basis of data collected from primary sources alone.

SCHEME OF THE STUDY

The Chapter I presents the theme of the study, review of the literature and need for the study. The objectives of the study and hypotheses to be tested are also specified, the limitations of the study are presented at the end.

The Chpater II descusses the methodology adopted for the study. Sampling procedure, selection of study area, selection of sample farmers, description of the study area, nature and source of data are presented. Then a comprehensive discussion on analytical methods used in the study is also specified.

It is in Chapter III, the trends in area, production and productivity of coconut plantation are explained at the

National, State and District levels. Coconut development in India during various five year plans is also discussed.

The cost of cultivation is attempted in Chapter IV. After a brief profile of sample farmers, a discussion on cost of cultivation in irrigated and unirrigated farms among small, medium and large farmers is done. Inferences drawn are presented at the end.

The Chapter V presents the analysis of production of coconut in the study area. Total production and productivity of the sample farmers, and production of tender, desiccated coconut and copra in case of different size groups of farmers in the study area are discussed.

The Chapter VI discusses the marketing of coconut in Tumkur District. In this Chapter, cost per acre, gross returns, net profits per acre and output-input ratio in coconut cultivation are estimated. Before that, trends in sales and prices of coconut in two Agricultural Produce Market Committees (APMC) in Tumkur district forms has been carried out in case of irrigated and unirrigated holdings.

The Chapter VII presents the summary of the findings and conclusions.

REFERENCES

1. Pethiyagoda, U: *Hand book on coconut cultivation*, Coconut Research Institute of Sri Lanka, Lunuwila, 1982, pp. 1- 5.
2. Markose, V.T.: *Coconut Development in India*, Coconut Development Board, Bangalore, Karnataka, India, 1980, pp. 701 - 707.
3. Thampan, P.K.: *Glimpses of Coconut Industry in India*, Coconut Development Board, Government of India, Cochin, 1988, pp. 1-214.
4. Child, R.: *Coconuts*, Longman Group Ltd., London, 1974, pp. 217 - 220.
5. Gopalan: The coconut palm, *Indian Coconut Journal*, Vol, 7, No.8, 1954, pp. 15 - 52.
6. ________: Improvement of the coconut crop by selection, *Malya Agricultural Journal*, Vol.20, No.18, 1951, pp. 30 - 39.
7. Mandal, R.C.: *Coconut production and protection Technology*, Agro Botanical Publishers, India, 1991, pp. 1 - 155.
8. John, M.C.: Coconut cultivation, ICAR Publishers, New Delhi, 1970, pp. 1 - 50.

09. Patel, J.S.: The coconut - a monograph, Govt. Press, Madras, 1938, 99 1 - 30.
10. Sampson, H.C.: The Coconut palm, Jone Balesons and Deniels Son Ltd., London, 1923, pp. 1 - 62.
11. Thampan, P.K.: Profitable Coconut Growing, Coconut Development Board, Ministry of Agriculture, Govt. of India, Cochin, Kerala, 1984, pp. 1 - 58.
12. Punnathara, C.J. : "Cost of production of wheat in Punjab during the 1973-74 crop reason", Punjab Agricultural University, Ludhiana, Agricultural situation in India, Vol. 12 No. 6, 1975, pp. 441 - 443.
13. Subba Rao, K.: Rice Marketing system and compulsory levies in Andhra Pradesh - A Study of Public intervention in food grain marketing, Allied Publishers Pvt. Ltd., 1978, pp. 1 - 173 + xvi.
14. Ratna Reddy, V.: "New Technology in agriculture and changing size-productivity relationships: A study of Andhra Pradesh", Indian Journal of Agricultural Economics, Vol.48, No.4, 1993, pp. 633 - 648.
15. Rahman, M.H. and Kashem, M.A.: Growing and Marketing Problems of Pulse Crops in Bangla Desh", Economic Affairs, Vol.11, No.8, 1993, pp. 24 - 30.
16. Madappa, P.P.: A study of cost of production of coffee in India, Indian Journal of Agriculture, Vol. 25, No.4, 1967, pp. 16 - 26.
17. Das, P.K. : Estimating production costs and Returns for coconut in Kerala, Journal of Plantation Crops, Vol.12, No.2, 1994, pp. 152 - 159.
18. Latha Bastine, C. and Abdurazak, M.P. : Costs and returns in different sizes of coconut holdings in Northern Kerala, India, Journal of Plantation Crops, vol.18, No.4, 1984, pp. 369 - 372.
19. Nagaraj, N., Sastry, K.N.R. and Chndrakanth: Economic considerations in selecting coconut enterprise. Department of Agricultural Sciences, Bangalore, Karnataka, India, Journal of Plantation Crops, Vol.15, No.1, 1987, pp. 15 - 22.
20. Jakhade, V.M. and Kurian, A.P.: Credit needs for manuring coconut palms in Kerala, R.B.I. Bulletin, Vol. 23, No.9, 1969, pp. 1414 - 27.
21. Chandan Mukherjee: Optimal Strategy for replantation of coconut trees in Kerala, Centre for Development Studies, Uller, Trivendrum, India, 1975, pp. 10 - 1127.
22. Herath, H.M.G.: Economics of the holdings development approach in coconut: Some preliminary results, Journal of Plantation Crops, Vol.26, No.6, 1986, pp. 88 - 93.

23. Dalvi, H.I. and others: Price spread in the marketing of coconuts in Konkan region of Maharashtra State, Journal of Plantation Crops, Vol.15, No.1, 1986, pp. 30 - 48.
24. Mathew, C. : Summer irrigation to coconut palms, Coconut Bull. Indian, N.S. Vol.5, No.12, 1972, pp. 2 - 3.
25. Nambiar, C.K.B. and Joshi, O.P.: Apply organic manure to reduce coconut mortality on coastal sands, central plantation crops research Institute, Kasargod, Kerala, Indian Farming, Vol.34, No.5, 1984, pp. 221 - 22.
26. Viswanathan Pillai's : Coconut the vertile Crop of Kerala, Southern Economists, Vol.14, No.14, 1975, pp. 24 - 26.
27. Krishnaji, N. and Chandan Mukherji and others: Economic of Inter and mixed Cropping in the coconut gardens of Kerala, Some preliminary findings, Journal of Plantation Crops, Vol. 12, No.8, 1976, pp. 146 - 52.
28. Kunikrishnan: Coconut, The tree of health, Yojana, Vol.21, No.6, 1977, pp. 4 - 9.
29. Gita Aravamutham: Stunted Coconut Economy, Economics and Political Weekly, Vol.13, No.19, 1978, Kerala, pp. 15 - 18.
30. Jamool Unni: Changes in the Cropping pattern in Kerala, Some evidences on substitution of coconut for Rice, 1960-61 to 1978-79, Economics and Political Weekly, Vol.6, No.2, 1973, pp. 252 - 69.
31. Mohan, T.C.: Declining coconut Economics of Kerala - An analysis, Southern Economist, Vol.28, No.26, 1988, pp. 29 - 32.
32. Narayan and others: Coconut Development in Kerala, Expert evaluation, Centre for Development Studies, Trivendrum, 1991, pp. 1 - 56.
33. George, M.V. and Joseph, P.T. : A scheme for stabilization of coconut prices in Kerala, Southern Economist, Vol.12, No.16, 1973, pp. 25 - 26.
34. Thampan, P.K.: Promoting product diversification and by products utilization in coconut industry in India, Coconut Development Board, Ministry of Agriculture, Govt. of India, Cochin, Kerala, 1987, pp. 33 - 42.
35. Raveendra, P. : Demand, consumption pattern and consumer acceptability of desiccated coconut, Coconut Development Board, Ministry of Agriculture, Govt. of India, Cochin, Kerala, 1987, pp. 122 - 124.

36. Narasimhappa, C.: Processing and marketing of coconut and its products, Processing and Marketing of coconuts in India, Coconut Development Board, Ministry of Agriculture, Govt. of India, Cochin, Kerala, 1987, pp. 129 - 132.
37. Rebello, N.S.P., Chengappa, P.G. and Lalitha Achoth: An analysis of Arrivals and prices of coconuts in principal coconut markets in Karnataka, Coconut Development Board, Ministry of Agriculture, Govt. of India, Cochin, Kerala, 1987, pp. 142 - 143.

CHAPTER 2

METHODOLOGY, DATA BASE AND PROFILE OF THE STUDY AREA

This Chapter presents the methodology adopted for the study. It presents the characteristics of study region, the sampling technique, analytical methods used, nature and source of data. Then follows a brief profile of the study area.

SELECTION OF STUDY AREA

To evaluate the objectives of the study, a case study has been undertaken. Selection of Tumkur district as the study area among the 19 districts of Karnataka is due to the fact that it has the highest area under coconut cultivation and productivity of the crop as compared to other districts. It has an area of 65002[1] hectares of land under coconut cultivation and has productivity for exceeding other districts. A multiusage sampling design was adopted to select talukas, villages and farmers. In the first stage two talukas were selected, in the second stage four villages were selected and in the third stage farmers growing coconut trees were selected.

Tumkur is a taluka as well as a district headquarters in Karnataka, situated along Honnavar-Bangalore State Highway and also Bangalore-Pune National Highway. The town is also connected to Bangalore and Pune by railway line. Thus it has an easy access to various important marketing centres has an easy access to various important marketing centres both inside and outside the State.

Coconut is cultivated on commercial scale in Tumkur district. It ranks first in respect of area and production in Karnatka state. Tumkur district contributes about 46.51

percent to the total production of coconut in Karnataka (Table - 3.8). Coconut crop has acquired commercial importance in the district because of suitable climate and soil conditions. These reasons led to the choice of Tumkur district as the area of study.

SELECTION OF SAMPLE TALUKAS

The large scale cultivation of coconut is mainly concentrated in Tiptur taluka occupying an area of 16384 hectares forming about 25.21 percent of the total area under coconut in the district. And Chikanayakanahalli tluka occupying an area of 15381 hectares has about 23.66 percent of the total area under coconut in the district (Table - 3.11). Therefore, Tiptur and Chikanayakanahalli talukas were purposely selected for the study out of 10 talukas of the district.

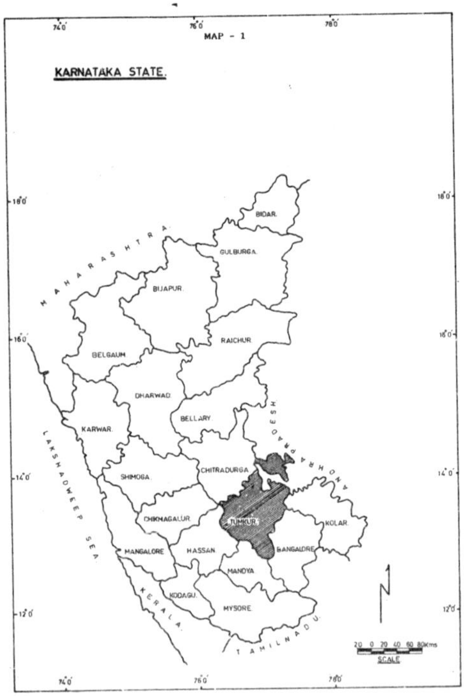

Map 1

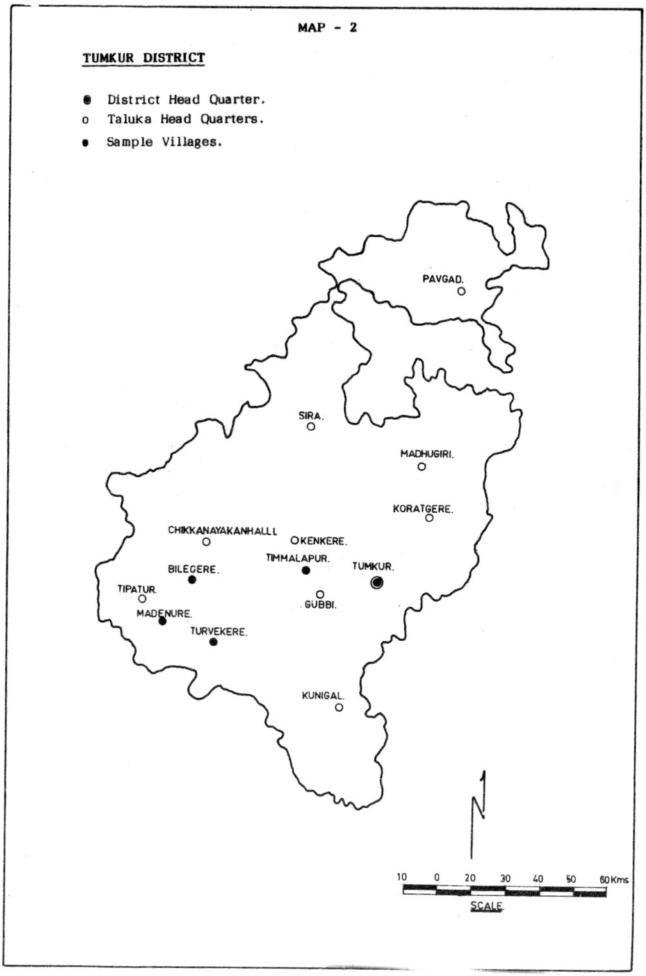

Map 2

SELECTION OF VILLAGES

There are 222 and 226 villages in Tiptur and Chikanayakanahalli taluka as per 1991 census. The list of villages cultivating coconut in Chikanayakanahalli and Tiptur taluka during 1994-95 reason was obtained from the offices of the Assistant Director of Agriculture at Tiptur and Chikanayakanahalli. Village Accountants of of the Revenue Department who have direct contact with the farmers of various villages in the talukas were also consulted to gather information about villages cultivating coconut to on large scale. On the basis of information gathered from the Village Accountants and the list obtained from Assistant Director of Agriculture, two villages were selected at random from each taluka. The names of the selected villages are (i) Madenur, (ii) Biligere from Tiptur taluka and (iii) Kenkere, (iv) Thimlapura from Chikanayakanahalli taluka.

All the four villages are situated along Bangalore-Honnavar Highway. They have more or less same agro-climatic conditions. The total area of Madenur is 952 hecates, Biligere 900.34 hectares, Kenkere 984 hectares and Thimlapura is having 816 hectares. Population of these four villages is not given separately in the 1991 census and the same is being included in the population of Tiptur and Chikanayakanahalli Municipal Councils. Though Madenur, Biligere, Kenkere, Thimplapura are villages, they are not less important than any of the town areas, the reason being that they are very near to the big- towns viz., Chikanayakanahalli and Tiptur. All the villages have frequent private buses and transport facilities. A branch of Gramina Bank if working in Biligere, Kenkere providing credit to farmers of the villages. Both the talukas have Agricultural Produce Marketing Committee (APMC) yard, Chikanayakanahalli has newly constructed Agricultural Produce Marketing Committee (APMC) yard.

SELECTION OF SAMPLE FARMERS

The farmers of the sample villages were divided into three groups, based on the size of their land holdings, namely, small (upto 5 acres) medium (above 5 and upto 10 acres) and large (above 10 acres). The list of farmers with the size of land owned was obtained from the records available with the Village Accountants of respective villages. The study intends to find the estimates of cost of cultivation of coconut, production, productivity and income derived by the coconut growers in each group and also their variation from one group to another. Also the average size of coconut plantation among the majority of farmers in the study area is ranged from one area to five acres. Therefore in each group (small, medium and large). 10 farmers were selected at random from the selected villages. Thus 30 farmers from each village were selected at random. In all, 120 sample farmers from the four selected villages were chosen for detailed investigation on various aspects of cost of cultivation, production, productivity of coconut garden, income derived, marketing of coconut etc.

For evaluating the objectives of the study necessary primary data were obtained from the selected farmers through personal interview method during October 1995. With the help of pre-tested and structured schedule, farmers were asked questions in local kannada language. The data so collected refer to the agricultural year, 1994-95. Most of the farmers had not maintained the records, receipts and expenditure on various aspects of coconut cultivation. Hence the collection of data is based on the recall method on the basis of enquiry made with the farmers of the study area.

The data collected from the farmers are related to preparation of land, seeds used, costs incurred on the purchase of various inputs, total production and its costs, the time of sale, price received and marketing of coconut etc.

In addition to primary data collected from sample formers, secondary data were also obtained. Secondary data on area, production, yield and prices, etc., of coconut at district and state levels were also collected form Bureau of Economics and Statistics. Talukawise area under coconut in Tumkur district, land use pattern etc., were obtained from District Statistical Office. Data on yearly prices of coconut were obtained from Agricultural Produce Marketing Committee, Tiptur and Chikanayakanahalli.

ESTIMATES OF GROWTH RATES

To find out the growth rates area, production, productivity of coconut crop, the following form of trend equation is used at the National, State and District level.

Y = ABtV .... (1)

Where,

Y = Area of production or productivity in the year 't'.

A & B = are parameters

A = Intercept indicating the value of Y in the base period t.

t = Time period starting from 1980-81 to 1994-95.

V = Error term.

Percent of growth rate can be calculated as

r = (Antilog B-1) x 100 where,

r = Average annual compound growth rate.

Equation (1) is converted into the logarithmic form in order to facilitate the use of linear equation. Taking logarithm on both sides of equation we get,

$$\text{Log } Y = \text{Log } A + t(\log B) + \text{Log } V$$

or

$$y = a + bt + v \quad \text{.................................} \quad (2)$$

Where,

$y = \log Y$, $b = \log B$, $a = \log A$, $v = \log V$.

The linear equation of above form is used for estimating annual compound growth rate of area, production and productivity of coconut crop grown in National, State and District levels. The value of a and b are estimated by using ordinary least squares method for the period 1980 to 1995.

COST OF PRODUCTION, RETURNS AND PROFITS

Tabular analysis of data is followed to identify and compare the costs, returns and profits among different size-groups of farmers for irrigated and unirrigated areas. The cost of production, returns and profits for coconut crop are computed as follows:

Cost of Production

The total cost of production (TC) at the farm gate has been calculated for the coconut crop as follows:

Total cost of Production (TC)* = Material Cost(A) + Labour Cost(B) + Irrigation Cost(C)

$$TC = A + B + C$$

Cost A:

Material Cost includes cost incurred on seeds, manure, fertilizer and pesticides. These were valued at the purchase

* The rental value of the land is not taken into account while computing the cost of production for both the irrigated and unirrigated crop because the farmers interviewed by the researcher were all owner cultivators.

rate for the year 1994-95. The value of owned things such as manure, seeds were valued at the prevailing market price. The rate was inclusive of hire charges of transport of seeds, manure, fertilizer and pesticides to fields.

Cost B

Labour charges included the wages paid to bullock and human labour used for all agricultural operations starting from preparation of land till the harvesting of crop. These agricultural operations for which farmers paid wages, are land preparation and ploughing, harrowing, manuring, planting, fertilizer application, hand weeding, intercultivation, application of chemicals etc. Daily wages, prevailing in the study area, paid to both men and women were taken into account. And wages for bullocks labour were taken into account for a pair of bullock and a person needed to operate the bullock pair. It was valued at the rate of hire charges per day prevailing in the study area.

Cost C

Irrigation cost included costs such as per irrigation charges, pot watering of coconut etc. The cost of irrigation refers to the apportioned cost of installation of wells, pumphouse, pumps and repairs which are assumed to serve for long period. In the long run there are no fixed costs and all costs will be variable costs.

Returns, Profit and Output-Input Ratio

Returns and profits are computed as follows:

$$\text{Gross Return} = \text{Total output} \times \text{price}$$

Gross returns are obtained multiplying the total output of individual sample farmer and price received by him for coconut during the year 1994-95. Average gross returns per acre are also obtained for small, medium and large holdings. It is to be noted that the gross return is calculated on the basis of the output marketed by the farmers in case of coconut, as the domestic consumption of coconut in the study area is found to be negligible.

Profit or net income is arrived at deducting cost of production from the gross returns.

Profit or Net Income = Gross Returns – Total Cost of Production

Output - input ratio in case of irrigated and unirrigated coconut crop is worked out dividing output (returns) by input (cost). Output-input ratio equal to one shows that there is no profit and no loss in the cultivation of the crop. Output-input ratio below one shows loss to the producer and above one shows profit. With increase in the ratio above one, there is a corresponding increase in profit also. This output-input ratio shows the extent of profit or loss in the cultivation of coconut crop in irrigated and unirrigated areas. Comparing the output-input ratio in irrigated and unirrigated areas, it becomes possible to know that in which area the coconut cultivation is more profitable.

THE DATA BASE

It is already detailed in the methodology that the first source of data is the producers of coconut collected from the sample of 120 farmers. In addition to this, the secondary data on various aspects of coconut are gathered from the Central Plantation Crops Research Institute, Kasargod, Centre for Development Studies, Trivendrum. The Directorate of Agricultural Marketing, Bangalore, was another basic source from whom the data on prices, market arrivals and market sales were collected. The various publications of The Directorate of Economics and Statistics (DES), and other periodicals, have been referred to in the study wherever necessary. Lastly, field notes of the researcher while on study is yet another resource material for aiming at an accurate, analytical and indepth study of the cost of cultivation, production and productivity, and marketing of coconut. Since coconut is a perennial crop of 6 to 7 years, information on establishment and maintenance of coconut garden for long period is required. For this study, sample farmers of different size groups in both irrigated and unirrigated garden in the Tumkur district were taken as a case study. The records of certain farmers were maintained satisfactorily, while in case of others not so. However, the study is largely based on the information provided by the farmers based on farmer's experience.

PROFILE OF THE STUDY AREA

General Introduction

Tumkur is one of the nineteen districts of the Karnataka State, and is situated in the east-central part of the State and to the south and south east of Chitradurga district. With an eventful history and rich cultural traditions, the district is also bestowed with natural resources. The western part consists of hills running approximately in a south-easternly directioin and eastern part of the district is occupied by a narrow range of granitic hills. The forest region in the district is under the dry-belt zone as district form the ever green and the mixed-belt which are found in the extreme west of old Mysore area. The boundary limit between the dry-belt zone and the mixed-belt zone is seen near the eastern slopes. The forest regions in the district are found to a large extent in the lower slopes of hills ranges. The rainfall increases from north to south generally, and in the western part of the district from the west to the east. There are a few small rivers and a number of big streams that rise in the hills and feed number of tanks. The west-eastern parts consist of an open area with attractive lake and stony hills[2].

The administrative headquarters of this district is Tumkur. There are various traditional derivations of the name Tumkur. The name is written and pronounced in Kannada as Tumme-Ooru or Tumbe-Ooru and its anglicized form is Tumkur[3].

Location

Tumkur belongs to the group of districts called the maidan (plains) district and is situated in the east-central part of the Karnataka State and to the south and south-east of Chitradurga district. It is situated between 12°45' and 14°20' north longitude and between 76°20' and 77°31' east longitude[4].

Boundary

On the boundaries of the district, it has on the north the Anantapur district of Andhra Pradesh, on the east, the Kolar and Ban galore districts, on the south, the Mandya district and on the west, the districts of Chitradurga, Chikmagalur and Hassan[5].

There are at present 10 revenue talukas in the district. These talukas are grouped into revenue sub-divisions, for administrative purposes viz., Tumkur sub-division, Tiptur sub-division and Madhugeri sub-division.

Area, Population and Density

Tumkur district covers an area of 10596 sq. kms. which is 5.5 percent of the states total area. According to the 1991 census, the population of the district is 23,05819 and it accounts for 0.51 percent of the states population. Of the total population, rural population accounts for 82.8 percent and urban population about 17.2 percent. The density of population is 218 per sq. km[6].

There are 10 talukas and 10 taluka panchayat boards, one municipality and 6 town municipalities. The district administration centre is in Tumkur city and it is 72 kms away from the capital city- Bangalore. Of the total area of the district, Sira taluka covers 1551 sq. kms., which is 14.64 percent of the total area and it is the biggest taluka in the district[7]. The talukawise area of the district is given in the Table 2.1.

Table 2.1 : Talukawise Area of Tumkur District

Sl. No.	Taluka	Area (in Square Kilometers)	Percentage
1.	Sira	1551	14.64
2.	Chiknayakanahalli	1113	10.51
3.	Gubbi	1221	11.52
4.	Korategere	652	6.15
5.	Kunigal	981	9.26
6.	Madhugeri	1131	10.67
7.	Pavagada	1358	12.82
8.	Tiptur	785	7.41
9.	Tumkur	1026	9.68
10.	Turvekere	778	7.34
	Total	10596	100.00

Source: Tumkur District At a Glance 1994-95. District Statistical Office, Tumkur 1995, pp 8-9.

According to 1991 population census the total population in the district was about 2305819 and out of this, male population was about 1177233 and female population was about 1128586. The density of population in the district is 218 per sq. km. Tumkur taluka has high density of population i.e. 415 per sq. km. and Pavagada taluka has low density of population which is 151 per sq. km[8].

Agriculture and Agricultural Development

According to the village records, the area of the district is about 1064755 hectares. Out of this, forest covers an area of 44984 hectares (4.23%). The land used for cultivation is about 81441 hectares (7.65%), barren land and the land which is not suitable for cultivation is 67539 hectares (6.34%), barren land used for cultivation is 66388 hectares (6.23%) and the other grass lands 104884 hectares (9.85%)[9].

In the year 1994-95, the total sown area in the district was 634146 hectares. It was 580372 hectares in 1993-94. The net sown area was 560449 hectares, whereas it was 575083 hectares in the previous year. In 1994-95 the land suitable for cultivation was 66388 hectares[10].

Table 2.2 : Net Sown Area in Different Talukas of Tumkur District, 1994-95.

Sl. No.	Name of Taluka	Area (in hectares)	Percentage
1.	Chiknayakanahalli	53320	9.51
2.	Gubbi	64405	11.49
3.	Korategere	37504	6.69
4.	Kunigal	54393	9.71
5.	Madhugeri	56921	10.61
6.	Pavagada	73165	13.05
7.	Sira	71788	12.81
8.	Tiptur	49324	8.80
9.	Tumkur	53604	9.56
10.	Turvekere	46025	8.21
	Total	560449	100.00

Source: Tumkur District At a Glance 1994-95. District Statistical Office, Tumkur 1995, pp 6-9.

Table 2.3: Distribution of Land-Holdings in Tumkur District During 1994-95

Name of Taluka	Size of Holdings (in hectares)										
	Less than 1 hectare		Between 1 & 2 hectares		Between 2 & 4 hectares		Between 4 & 10 hectares		Above 10 hectares		Total
	Area	Percentage to the Total Area	Area	Percentage to the Total Area	Area	Percentage to the Total Area	Area	Percentage to the Total Area	Area	Percentage to the Total Area	
1. Chiknayaka-nahalli	10070	15.79	16107	25.25	17993	28.21	16146	25.31	3468	5.44	63784
2. Gubbi	14174	18.86	19980	26.58	20460	27.22	16555	22.03	3992	5.31	75161
3. Korategere	7053	16.03	11832	26.89	12868	29.24	9739	22.13	2517	5.72	44009
4. Kunigal	12699	20.29	15796	25.24	16625	26.56	14101	22.53	3368	5.38	62589
5. Madhugeri	10266	14.96	17075	24.88	18811	27.41	16055	23.39	6422	9.36	68629
6. Pavagada	4384	4.37	10269	10.24	15901	15.86	33081	33.00	36603	36.52	100238
7. Sira	6012	6.37	16679	17.68	24044	25.48	32198	34.13	15419	16.34	94352
8. Tiptur	9902	18.24	13380	24.65	14627	26.94	13152	24.23	3228	5.95	54289
9. Tumkur	12565	17.66	17398	24.45	19599	27.55	17096	24.03	4487	6.31	71145
10. Turvekere	11551	21.22	14621	26.86	14906	27.39	11011	20.23	2340	4.30	54429
TOTAL	98676 (14.33)		153137 (22.24)		175834 (25.53)		179134 (26.01)		81844 (11.89)		688625 (100)

Source: Tumkur District At a Glance 1994-95. District Statistical Office, Tumkur 1995, pp 15-17.

Table 2.4: Area Under Major Crops in the Tumkur District During 1994-1995

Talukas	Paddy		Ragi		Jawar		Bajra		Wheat		Hybrid Jawar		Other cereals		Tur		Other pulses		Ground Nut		Sugarcane		Cotton	
	Area	%	Area	%	Area	%	Area	%	Area	%	Area	%	Area	%	Area	%	Area	%	Area	%	Area	%	Area	%
1*	1937	5.34	20059	12.15	2090	20.62	160	19.54	-	-	4	0.10	1031	15.31	1056	11.16	8349	12.38	1864	1.03	-	-	28	3.91
2	3819	10.42	30101	18.23	415	4.09	19	2.32	-	-	405	10.61	205	3.04	999	10.56	8500	12.60	5675	58.65	154	5.32	3	0.42
3	2039	5.56	8600	5.21	253	2.50	2	0.24	-	-	471	12.34	168	2.50	562	5.94	3203	4.75	22870	12.70	216	7.46	-	-
4	9307	25.39	29089	17.62	-	-	-	-	-	-	43	1.13	120	1.78	465	4.92	9161	13.58	532	2.95	524	18.11	-	-
5	2827	7.71	5861	3.55	152	1.50	3	0.37	15	25.00	2315	60.67	726	10.78	837	8.85	6445	9.56	37108	20.5	1425	49.24	1	0.14
6	1625	4.43	1845	1.11	754	7.44	252	30.77	2	3.33	15	0.39	460	6.83	2766	29.24	4835	7.17	59730	33.15	63	2.18	38	5.30
7	2572	7.02	5759	3.49	2012	19.85	410	5.06	-	-	27	0.71	4780	56.13	940	9.94	5863	8.67	45808	25.42	416	14.37	550	76.71
8	1181	3.22	20784	12.59	2040	20.13	-	-	43	71.67	57	1.50	50	0.74	490	5.18	7439	11.03	383	0.21	-	-	95	13.25
9	8715	23.78	23607	14.30	565	5.57	-	-	-	-	270	7.00	26	0.39	809	8.55	6973	10.34	5388	2.99	69	2.38	2	0.28
10	2614	7.13	19404	11.75	1855	18.30	-	-	-	-	209	5.48	168	2.49	535	5.66	6675	9.90	828	0.46	27	0.93	-	-
TOTAL	36656	100	165109	100	10136	100	819	100	60	100	3816	100	6734	100	9459	100	67443	100	180186	100	2894	100	717	100

Source: Government of Karnataka, Tumkur District At a Glance 1994-95. District Statistical Office, Tumkur 1995, pp. 20-22.

* Serial numbers refer to Talukas in the District and they are in the same order as presented in Table 2.3

It is clear from the Table 2.02 that out of the ten talukas in the district, Pavagada taluka has the largest portion of the total net sown area covering 13.05 percent of the total 560449 hectares. Sira taluka has 12.81 percent followed by Tumkur, Gubbi and Kunigal talukas with 9.56, 11.49 and 9.71 percent respectively. Chinayakanahalli, Madhugeri, Tiptur and Turvekere talukas are with 9.51, 10.16, 8.80 and 8.21 percent respectively. Whereas Koratagere taluka accounts for only 6.69 percent the net sown area in the district, in the year 1994-95[11].

An horizontal analysis of the Table 2.03 shows that out of the total land holdings constituting 688265 hectares, most of the talukas on an average, have an increasing trend in area in the size group of one hectare to 4 hectares. However, as an exception, Pavagada taluka has the reverse trend where in the largest area i.e. 35.52 percent of the total area is under big holdings.

Cropping Pattern

It is found that ground nut is the major crop in the district covering an area of 180186 hectares, followed by ragi with an area of 165109 hectares (Table 2.04). The third major crop in the district is the pulses covering an area of 67443 hectares, followed by paddy with 36656 hectares. Jowar covers an area of hectares, followed by paddy with 36656 hectares. Jowar covers an area of 10136 hectares. Hybrid jowar, bajra, cotton, sugarcane and wheat have an area below 5,000 hectares but form important crops in the district. However, wheat is the only crop which is grown only in three talukas in the district and rest of the crops on an average have an equal distribution in almost all the talukas excepting very few.

Coconut Cultivation in Tumkur District

Coconut cultivation in Tumkur district covers about 65002 hectares of land constituting 11.60 percent of the total net sown area in the district, Tiptur taluka alone accounts for about 25.21 percent of the total area under coconut cultivation in the district. Talukawise distribution of the area under coconut with percentage to the total area under coconut in the district for the year 1995-96 is given in Table 2.05.

Table 2.5 : Talukawise Distribution of Area Under Coconut in Tumkur District, 1995-96

Sl. No.	Name of Taluka	Area (in hectares)	Percentage to Total Area under Coconut
1.	Chiknayakanahalli	15381	23.66
2.	Gubbi	11380	17.51
3.	Kunigal	2650	4.08
4.	Tiptur	16389	25.21
5.	Tumkur	6320	9.72
6.	Turvekere	10040	15.45
7.	Pavagada	250	0.38
8.	Madhugeri	635	0.98
9.	Sira	1264	1.94
10.	Korategere	698	1.07
	Total	65002	100.00

Source: Tumkur District At a Glance 1995-96. District Statistical Office, Tumkur 1996, pp 6-7.

Coconut forming has been very important activity in the district because of the extent of acreage and quality of the nuts. Tumkur district has an extensive acreage under the crop. Tiptur, Chiknayakanahalli and Gubbi talukas have large areas under coconut and the nuts gathered from these places are sold throughout the State. Out of the total acreage in the entire district, three talukas namely Tiptur, Chiknayakanahalli, Gubbi and Turvekere account for a lion share.

Irrigation

According to the natural divisions, the source of irrigation also varies. There are two important rivers in the district namely Shimsha and Jayamangali. A number of streams, tanks and wells of the district are utilised for irrigational purposes. It is called granary of Karnataka as there is an assured supply of water, particularly to main season crops. Anicut and reservoirs have been constructed for irrigation purpose. They include the Sankanapura anicut constructed across the Nagini river in Kunigal taluka, the Macronahalli reservoir project at Amruthur in which was constructed as a famine relief work across the Swarnamukhi river. A new reservoir has been constructed across the Nagini river near Mangala in Kunigal taluka[12].

Table 2.6 : Different Sources of Irrigation in Tumkur District During 1994-95

Taluka	Cannal		Tank		Well		Borewell		Others		Total	
	Area	%	*Area*	%	*Area*	%	*Area*	%	*Area*	%		
1. Chiknaya kanahalli			1132	3.40	363	1.14	1649	11.37	-	-	3144	3.92
2. Gubbi			4781	14.35	2124	6.67	1909	13.16	-	-	8814	11.00
3. Korategere			4924	14.78	1958	6.15	1721	11.87	-	-	8603	10.74
4. Kunigal			5735	17.22	2334	7.33	595	4.10	141	63.80	8805	10.99
5. Madhugeri			4579	13.75	7663	24.06	2611	18.00	-	-	14853	18.54
6. Pavagada			746	2.24	5573	17.50	391	2.70	10	4.53	6720	8.39
7. Sira	240	100	5600	16.81	5565	17.47	218	1.50	70	31.67	11693	14.58
8. Tiptur			370	1.11	460	1.44	1237	8.54	-	-	2067	2.58
9. Tumkur			3512	10.54	40560	12.73	3230	22.27	-	-	10798	13.48
10. Turvekere			1932	5.80	1756	5.51	941	6.49	-	-	4629	5.78
TOTAL	240 (0.30)		33311 (41.57)		31852 (39.75)		14502 (18.09)		221 (0.03		80126 (100)	

Source: Tumkur District At a Glance 1994-95. District Statistical Office, Tumkur 1995, pp 19-20.

The district has a large number of tanks. Kunigal taluka has the largest irrigated area under tanks, as the two large irrigation reservoirs are constructed in the taluka. Open wells and bore wells are also in large numbers, though surface irrigation is the major source of irrigation in the ditrict.

Net irrigated area in the year 1994-95 was about 80126 hectares. Out of the net irrigated area, the area served by canals was 240 hectares, tank irrigation 33311 hectares, well irrigation about 31852 hectares, borewells 14502 hectares and by others about 221 hectares. Talukawise different sources of irrigation in the district is presented in the Table 2.06.

Horticulture and Plantation Crops

Horticulture, though a part of agriculture in general, has been receiving separate and special attention since 1970's in the district. The cultivation of fruit and vegetable crops was encouraged and efforts were made to popularize the importance of horticultural products as a source of quality food.

Fruit crops are grown in almost all the talukas in the district, and plantains (banana), mangoes and grapes are important fruit crops raised in the district. Mangoes and plantains are grown in all the talukas of the district especially in Tumkur, Kunigal, Chiknayakanahalli and Gubbi talukas. Vegetable crops like onions and potatoes are also grown to some extent in the district.

The Mysore Horticulture Society, which was started as early as in 1912, has opened branches in the taluka headquarters of the district to propagate the great need to grow more fruits and vegetables. The society provides facilities to the members by way of providing technical advice and supply of plants and seeds. Financial and technical assistance have been provided in order to increase the production of horticultural crops. Under a vegetable development scheme, technical guidance and good seeds have been provided. A few schemes have been under way in the district to intensify vegetable and fruit production in which plants and seeds are supplied at 5 percent concessional rates to the growers[13].

The importance of plantation crops in the district dates back to yester years. The major plantation crops in the district are coconut, Arecanut, Banana, Pepper, Fruits, etc. However, the coconut plantation is highly prominent in the district due to conducive climatic and soil conditions and sufficient irrigation facilities. As coconut has social, economic and religious importance not only in the district and the State but also in the whole nation, it is widely grown in coastal parts of the country. Among them, Tumkur district bags the first place both in production and area of coconut in the state. Moreover coconut economy contributes considerable share to the country's national income and provides gainful employment to many unskilled and semiskilled labourers. It has almost become source of livelihood for many Tumkurians. More so it has and is playing a significant role in improving economic conditions of many coconut growers in the district. Hence, the spread of coconut cultivation and its importance has attached the eyes of many researchers to the field.

Co-operation and Banking

In the year 1994-95, there were 1294 co-operative societies. Out of them, 238 Agricultural Co-operative Societies, 540 milk co-operatives and 413 other co-operatives societies. In the district 785000 members belong to these co-operative socieities[14].

In the district there are 10 primary Land Development Banks, 20 Co-operative Banks. Out of which 9 are Urban Co-operative Banks. There are 132 branches of Commercial Banks spread throughout the district and out of them 50 are in rural area[15].

During 1994-95 commercial banks have provided Rs.22,158 lakhs of credit against a deposit of Rs. 3,76,634 lakhs whereas the urban co-operative banks have provided Rs. 40.5 lakhs credit to agriculture[16].

Agrucultural Produce and Regulated Markets

For marketing of agricultural produce in the district there are 10 main markets and 20 sub-markets. During the year 1994-95 the total sale proceeds of agricultural produce in all the regulated markets was Rs. 141.19 crores. Out of which Tiptur taluka has the highest share of 53.49 percent, followed by Tumkur with 23.63 percent where in the remaining 25 percent of the sale proceeds is shared by other talukas in the district[17].

Climate, Rainfall and Soil

The climate of this district, excluding the northern most part, is similar to that of Bangalore district. But the climate of the Pavagada region and the part of the district north of Sira, is like that of the Chitradurga district with a somewhat hotter summer. Maximum temperature may some times reach 40 or 41°C. The year may be divided into four seasons. The dry season with clear bright weather is from December to February. The period from March to May constitutes the hot season and the south-west monsoon season is from June to September. October and November may be termed the post-monsoon season. December is generally the coolest month of the year. The daily minimum temperature in the cold season some times goes down to 9 to 10°C[18].

The average rainfall in the district is 688.4 mm. The rainfall increases from the north to the South generally, and in the western part of the district from the west to the east. The rainfall is mostly confined to the period from May to November. The rainfall during the south-west monsoon season is only 50 percent of the annual rainfall[19].

The soil in the district is generally hard and poor with the exception of land irrigated by tanks, nalas and canals, which are fertile. The red soil, which is known as the ragi soil is common in the southern and western talukas and the black soil is found to some extent in the northern talukas and the sandy soil is common in the eastern tracts. The net areas. Red gravelly sandy, clay loam, black soil, sandy loam, sandy clay, clay and alkaline soils are found in the district[20].

In Tumkur taluka there is abundant red loam soil, gravelly soil, sandy loam soil and clay soil. In Madhugeri taluka loam and black soils are found. Pavagada taluka has four types of soils namely, clammy soil, black soil, sandy loam soil and clay soil. Gravelly soil, black soil, sandy loam soil and clay soil are almost common in Tiptur. In Turvekere taluka five types of soils namely gravelly soil, sandy soil, clammy loam, block soil and clay soil are found. Chiknayakanahalli has gravelly soil, sandy soil and block soil. Korategere taluka has plenty of sandy soil. Sandy loam soil, clay soil and particularly alkaline which is not found in any of the talukas in the district. Whereas in Sira taluka almost all types of soil except clay and alkaline are found. The red and red loamy soils which are common throughout the district having good drainage are generally considered suitable for growing a wide variety of crops particularly coconut plantation.

REFERENCES

1. Government of Karnataka: Tumkur District At a Glance, 1994-95, District Statistical Office, Tumkur, pp. 2 - 3.
2. K. Abhishankara (Ed.), Mysore State, Tumkur District Gazetter, Directorate of Printing Stationery and Publications, Bangalore, 1996, p. 1.
3. *Ibid.*, p. 2.
4. *Ibid.*, p. 3.
5. *Ibid.*, p. 4.
6. District Statistical Office, Tumkur District At a Glance, 1994-95, District Statistical Office, Tumkur, pp. 8 - 9.
7. *Ibid.*, p. 17.
8. *Ibid.*, pp. 17 - 18.
9. *Ibid.*, p. 11.
10. *Ibid.*, p. 13.
11. *Ibid.*, p. 14.
12. K. Abhishankara (Ed.), *op.cit.*, p. 108.
13. *Ibid.*, p. 147.
14. Tumkur District At a Glance, 1994, *op.cit.*, p. 37.
15. *Ibid.*, p. 36.
16. *Ibid.*, p. 38.
17. *Ibid.*, p. 35.
18. K. Abhishankar (Ed), *op.cit.*, p. 20.
19. *Ibid.*, 21.
20. *Ibid.*, p 22.

CHAPTER 3

TRENDS IN AREA, PRODUCTION AND PRODUCTIVITY OF COCONUT

Before discussing in detail the economics of coconut plantation in Tumkur district, it is useful to analyse trends in area, production and productivity of coconut. Hence an analysis relating to trends in area, production and productivity at the national, state and district levels is presented in this chapter. Establishment of the coconut development board and the programmes for coconut development under plan periods are also discussed.

AREA UNDER COCONUT CULTIVATION, PRODUCTION AND PRODUCTIVITY IN DIFFERENT GROWING COUNTRIES OF THE WORLD

Coconut is a crop having great importance in India. It has recorded a history of over 300 years and has always been considered as the tree of leaves in the local tradition. "India is one of the largest coconut producing countries of the world. With an area of about 1.2 million hectares and an annual production of 5871 million nuts (1983), the country ranks third in the world map of coconut. The relative position the country in the world could be seen from the Table 3.1.

Coconut Development in India

Coconut in India is a crop of great importance. It is a crop with many uses. It is a source of food, drink and shelter to the humanity. Coconut is known as 'Kalpavruksha' or the tree of heaven in our country due to advantages and various uses the palm offers. It is valued both as a food crop and an oilseed. India ranks third in the world in coconut production, next to Philippines and Indonesia. The crop assumes great importance in the national economy from the view point of employment, income and export opportunities. It is essentially cultivated by small and marginal farmers of the coastal states of the country.

Table 3.1 : Area, Production and Productivity of Coconut in Different Countries

Years of refe- rence	Country	Area ('000 ha)	Perc- entage	Produ- ction	Perc- entage	Produ ctivity	No. of nuts per tonne of copra
1983	Philippines	3209	33.7	9666	29.0	3012	4500
1982	Indonesia	2923	30.7	8682	26.0	2970	4500
1983	India	1154	12.1	5871	17.6	5088	6800
1982	Sri Lanka	459	4.8	2521	7.5	5492	4925
1982	Thailand	418	4.4	663	2.0	1586	4450
1984	Malaysia	298	3.2	1399	4.2	4695	5270
1979	Papu New Guinea	265	2.8	1265	3.8	4774	5500
1973	Fiji	69	0.7	160	0.5	2319	600
1971	Zanzibar	49	0.5	154	0.3	3143	NA
1971	Trinidad and Tobago	12	0.1	86	0.2	7167	NA
1979	Western Sama	42	0.5	212	0.6	5048	5300
1975	Other areas	620	6.5	2700	8.1	-	NA
Total		9518	100.0	33379	100.0		

Source: P.K. Thampan, Coconut- The veritable source of food and oil, production symposium in Plantation opportunities in India, New Delhi, 31 Jan. - 1st Feb. 1986, pp. 81- 86.

Copra and coconut oil are the two traditional commodities in the domestic markets. Coconut oil commands a unique position as a premium priced oil for both edible as well as non-edible end uses. Six percent of the vegetable oil production in the country is accounted by coconut oil and is cherished especially by Keralites as a looking medium.

More than 10 million people depend directly or indirectly on the crop for their livelihood by its cultivation, processing, trade and industrial activities. The coir industry, which provides direct employment to more than 4 lakh workers derives its raw material from coconut. Export of coir and coir products earns foreign exchange to the tune of Rs. 100 crores every year. In the recent years various industrial units based on coconut kernel and coconut shell have come into existence creating wide employment opportunities to a sizeable section of the population and export opportunities.

Distribution of the Crop

Coconut is not grown in all the states of India, but is confined to coastal belts and certain interior tracts where the agro-climatic conditions favour its growth. It is grown continuously in the major coconut growing states of Kerala and in island groups such as Lakshadweep, Andaman and Nicobar Islands and Karaikal in union territory of Pondicherry. In other states it is confined to certain pockets accounting small area in each state. The four major coconut growing states viz., Kerala, Tamil Nadu, Karnataka and Andhra Pradesh together account for more than 91 percent of area under coconut in India. The small state in Kerala, with 5.8 percent of the area under coconut accounts for 41.9 percent of the production of coconut in India. The central, northern belts and some of the eastern states in the country are not so favourable for the cultivation of the crop due to their varied climatic conditions. Still there is scope for introduction of the crop atleast in some regons of Bihar, Madhya Pradesh and Tripura, Arunachal Pradesh and Nagaland[1].

Although India is one of the largest coconut producing countries of the world, the per capita availability of coconut in India is as low as 8 nuts per year whereas it is as high as 190 nuts in the Philippines, 56 nuts in Indonesia and 165 nuts in Sri Lanka[2]. Large population of India can be considered as the cause for such a low level of availability. It is also true that coconut is not grown in all states of the country. Coconut is grown in few states like Kerala, Tamil Nadu, Andhra Pradesh, Karnataka etc. and is required to meet the major domestic demand. As much as 56 percent of the total coconut area is concentrated in Kerala, a small state accounting for only 1.18 percent of the total area in the country. Karnataka State stands at the third place both in terms of area under production and productivity in the country. The Tumkur District deserves mention as it bags first place in Karnataka State in terms of area under coconut cultivation. Though the agro-climatic conditions in the central and northern belts in the country are not favourable for the introduction of this crop, in many states where it is only a minor crop, there is adequate scope for further expansion of the cultivation. The spread of coconut cultivation in the country is shown in Table 3.2.

Table 3.2 : State wise Area and Production of Coconut in India, 1991-92

State/Union Territories	Area ('000 ha)	Percentage	Production (Million nuts)	Percentage
Andhra Pradesh	63.4	4.2	959.2	9.6
Assam	9.8	0.6	78.9	0.8
Goa	24.0	1.6	110.0	1.1
Karnataka	238.2	15.7	1225.3	12.2
Kerala	846.3	55.8	4206.1	41.9
Maharashtra	7.9	0.5	121.5	1.2
Orissa	32.6	2.1	182.0	1.8
Tamil Nadu	240.3	15.8	2755.8	27.4
Tripura	7.0	0.5	4.2	0.0
West Bengal	19.8	1.3	263.3	2.6
A & N Islands	24.1	1.3	84.4	0.8
Lakshadweep	2.8	0.2	25.6	0.3
Pondicherry	1.8	0.1	26.9	0.3
All India	1518.0	100.0	10043.2	100.0

Source: Directorate of Economics and Statistics, Ministry of Agriculture, Govt. of India, 1992, pp 30-34.

Unlike other commercial crops grown in the country, coconut is essentially a small holdings crop. It is grown mostly in homestead gardens and small holdings. There are about 5 million coconut holdings in the country with 85 percent of such holdings occupying below two hectares. In Kerala alone there are about 2.5 million holdings. Details of the size of coconut holdings in the country are given in Table 3.03.

Table 3.3: Size of Coconut Holdings in Major Producing Sates

Size of Holding (in Ha)	Kerala	Tamil Nadu	Karnataka	Andhra Pradesh
Less than 0.2	37.1	69.1	52.5	56.5
0.2 - 1.0	52.8	26.0	42.9	41.7
1.0 - 2.0	7.9	3.2	3.6	1.8
2.0 and above	2.2	1.7	1.0	-

Source: Thampan P.K. Plantation Crops Opportunities and constraints, Oxford and IBH Publishing Co., New dehli, Bombay, Calcutta, 1991, pp 1 - 99.

The agricultural operations involved in the cultivation of coconut and the industries based on coconut are important sources of employment in the country. It is estimated that about 10 million people depend directly or indirectly on coconut culture and industry for their livelihood. The economy of the state of Kerala largely depends on the production of coconut. In Kerala coconut is the main stray of the people with the entire fabric of rural economy having closely woven around it. The contribution of the crop to the annual income of the state is around 15 percent and to the agricultural income is around 30 percent. The coconut related industries and other activities provided employment opportunities to millions of people in Kerala State and also sustained inter-state trading in coconut products amounting to a gross annual turnover of about Rs. 225 crores in the year 1982. Coconut cultivation makes a significant contribution to the national economy also.

TRENDS IN AREA PRODUCTION AND PRODUCTIVITY OF COCONUT IN INDIA

Coconut palm, one of the traditional tree crops grown in India, plays a vital role in the economic culture and social activities of the people, with an annual production of 9283 million nuts from an area of 1.5 million hectares during 1989-90. Cultivatoin of coconut in India is mostly concentrated in the west and east coasts of the country. The state of Kerala, which accounts for about one percent of the total land area of India, accounts for about 56.6 percent of the total area under coconut and contributes 47 percent of the production of coconut. The other Southern States viz. Tamil Nadu, Karnataka and Andhra Pradesh together account for 34 percent of area under coconut but contribute 44 percent of the production. The analysis of trends in area, production and productivity of coconut in India is discussed here with special reference to four major coconut growing states.

Table 3.4 : Area Under Coconut in Major Coconut Growing States in India

(in '000 hectares)

Year	Kerala	Karnataka	Tamil Nadu	Andhra Pradesh	Others	Total
1950-51	409.4	93.2	66.0	33.2	20.2	622.0
1955-56	448.0	88.3	51.5	35.6	23.6	647.0
1960-61	501.0	96.0	55.0	33.0	32.0	717.0
1965-66	586.3	115.4	90.2	33.3	59.5	884.0
1970-71	719.1	130.3	95.1	37.1	64.0	1045.5
1975-76	692.9	151.1	109.9	40.5	75.5	1069.9
1980-81	666.2	171.5	160.0	42.4	87.2	1083.3
1985-86	704.7	205.6	149.6	47.4	118.2	1225.6
1989-90	875.9	225.4	225.9	59.0	123.3	1509.5
Percentage increase in 1989-90 over 1950-51	113.9	141.8	242.3	77.7	510.4	142.7

Source: M.V. George and Others : *Coconut Journal*, Oct.-Nov. 1991, Vol. XXII.

The area under coconut showed an impressive growth during the period from 1955-56 to 1970-71, but the growth rate is slacked in the seventies and early eighties (Table 3.4). It is interesting to note that actually there was reduction in the area under coconut during the seventies and early eighties in Kerala, which resulted in lower growth rate in all India level. Due to the impact of root disease, the productivity of coconut gardens in the central and southern districts of Kerala has been steadily dwindling so that even well maintained coconut gardens have become less profitable and many cultivators in fact have preferred to replant coconut with rubber to get better returns. During 1976, more than 185 million bearing palms were estimated to be diseased in Kerala[3].

During the eighties efforts were made by the Central Plantation Crops Research Institute, Coconut Development Board and Department of Agriculture to find out solutions to the problems faced by the coconut farmers and these efforts proved to be fruitful and as a result the area under coconut cultivation started increasing, Coconut Development Board provided subsidies to farmers for coconut farming in new areas and this helped in reversing the declining trend in coconut acreage. Even in Karnataka there was no considerable increase during the fifties but a steady increase in the average production was noticed during the seventies and eighties. The only exception to this general trend is Andhra Pradesh where there was only marginal changes in area during the period 1950-71, but showed a slow but steady increase thereafter.

Table 3.5: Production of Coconut in Major Coconut Growing States in India

(in million nuts)

Year	Kerala	Karnataka	Tamil Nadu	Andhra Pradesh	Others	Total
1950-51	2026.0	369.0	463.0	306.0	418.0	3582
1955-56	3099.0	355.0	417.0	233.0	122.0	4226
1960-61	3220.0	498.0	448.0	297.0	176.0	4639
1965-66	3293.0	362.0	844.0	288.0	248.0	5035
1970-71	3981.0	731.8	941.5	157.0	263.7	6075
1975-76	3439.7	766.6	1098.6	173.4	352.0	5829
1980-81	3036.4	890.0	1132.8	175.3	486.7	5720
1985-86	3370.0	1062.0	1494.5	195.8	640.7	6770
1989-90	4394.0	1158.7	2302.4	654.7	773.2	9283
Percentage increase in 1989-90 over 1950-51	116.9	214.0	397.2	114.0	85.0	159.2

Source: M.V. George and Others : *Coconut Journal*, Oct.-Nov. 1991, Vol. XXII.

Table 3.5 shows the quinquennial changes in production of coconut in major producing states. The total production of coconut during 1950-51 was only 3582 million nuts which rose to 9283 million nuts was during 1989-90 recording an increase of 157 percent over a period of 40 years. It is interesting to note that there was a steep rise in the production of coconut in all the states during the period 1985 to 1990.

In Karnataka the production increased upto 1970-71 and then there was declining trend till 1980-81. This can be attributed mainly to the spread of root disease. George[4] estimated the loss in yield to be as high as 340 million nuts annually due to root and leaf diseases. Comprehensive survey conducted during 1984-85 by Central Plantation Crops Research Institute in collaboration with the Department of Agriculture, Coconut Development Board and five other agencies estimated a loss of 968 million nuts annually due to root disease. This severe loss in production of coconut in Kerala brought down the all India production of coconut also. However due to the concerned efforts of Coconut Development Board, Department of Agriculture and Central Plantation Crops Research Institute, the declining trend in production has been checked to some extent. As a result of well distributed rainfall from 1984-85 onwards, the production of coconut in Andhra Pradesh, Tamil Nadu and Kerala increased considerably which boosted the all India production to the level of 9283.4 million nuts during 1989-90.

In Andhra Pradesh, the production of coconut fluctuated and showed a declining trend till 1985-86 but showed a steep rise thereafter. The production of 195.8 million nuts recorded during 1985-86 which reached 654.7 million nuts during 1989-90. The low production level in Andhra Pradesh for 1970-71 to 1985-86 was mainly due to the frequent cyclone and the recurring droughts in the coconut growing areas. In Tamil Nadu, the production was around 400 million nuts during sixties. During seventies and eighties the production increased steadily with a steep increase during last four years. In Karnataka the total production of coconut was slowly increasing throughout the four decades except during the first half of sixties.

It can be observed from the Table 3.05 and 3.06 that the average productivity in India during 1950-51 was 5759 nuts per hectare which increased to 6532 nuts during 1955-56. Thereafter the productivity was found to be declining trend in all India productivity was mainly due to the declining trend in Kerala. During 1950-51, Kerala produced 2026 million nuts accounting for 57 percent in the national production which slipped down to 47 percent during 1989-90 though the actual production increased to 4394 million nuts during 1989-90. In Kerala, the average productivity of 6917 nuts during 1955-56 was highest and then decreased to 5617 nuts during 1975-76 and 1985-1986 respectively. The incidence of the debilitating disease like root and existence of larger areas under rainfed conditions resulted in the lower productivity in Kerala.

Table 3.6 : Productivity per Hectare in Major Coconut Growing States in India

Year	Kerala	Karnataka	Tamil Nadu	Andhra Pradesh	Total
1950-51	4949	3959	7015	9217	5759
1955-56	6917	4020	8097	6545	6532
1960-61	6427	5188	8145	9000	6470
1965-66	5617	3137	9357	8649	5698
1970-71	5536	5616	9900	4232	5811
1975-76	4964	5073	9996	4133	5449
1980-81	4558	5190	9762	4134	5280
1985-86	4792	5165	9990	4131	5524
1989-90	5017	5141	10192	11097	6150

Source: *Source*: M.V. George and Others : *Coconut Journal*, Oct.-Nov. 1991, Vol. XXII.

The increasing number of senile and unproductive palms in most of the holdings also exerted deleterious effect on the production and productivity of coconut in Kerala (Thampan, 1989)[5]. The survey conducted during 1984-85 covering the entire disease affected belt in Kerala revealed that the average yield per palm could be as high as 57 nuts whereas the usual state average was only 32 nuts. Irrigation can enhance the productivity of palms even in the severely disease affected regions. By improving irrigation facilities in coconut growing regions particularly in the northern districts of Kerala where the dry spell extends to 5 - 6 months, the productivity of palms can be enhanced considerably.

InKarnataka, the productivity per hectare was relatively low during the fifties and sixties with a dip during 1965-66 and reached the all India level during seventies and remained without much fluctuations. In Tamil Nadu, the productivity per hectare was always high, though fluctuating widely. The average productivity was almost double than that of Kerala. In Tamil Nadu, coconut is predominantly an irrigated crop. Wherever unirrigated crops are grown, the holdings are located near tanks and valleys where copious ground water supply to coconut root zone is available. It is interesting to note that the high average per hectare productivity in Tamil Nadu is also due to the high density of palms, which is about 319 palms per hectare. The corresponding figures for Kerala and Karnataka are 229 and 122, respectively. Though the average per palm yield in Karnataka is 54 nuts, the per hectare yield was low because of very low palm density. Whereas in Tamil Nadu with a low average yield of 44 nuts per palm, the productivity was found to be almost double than that of Kerala as well as the country as a whole.

The size and quality of nuts are also found varying from region to region. In Tamil Nadu, the main variety cultivated being the East Coast Tall, the size of the nuts is relatively small as compared to that of Kerala and hence the number of nuts per palm can be high. Another reason for the higher per palm productivity in Tamil Nadu and Karnataka is that a large number of nuts from these states are harvested within six months and consumed in the form of tender nuts. Whereas in Kerala the nuts are generally harvested after 11 or 12 months of maturity and as a result the per palm yield is low.

In Andhra Pradesh though the productivity was as high as 9217 nuts during 1950-51, it slipped down to 4232 nuts during 1970-71, but improved thereafter to 11097 nuts during 1989-90. Frequent cyclones with recurrent droughts were responsible for the low productivity during late sixties, seventies and early eighties.

Though there was considerable expansion in area under coconut and also in production in almost all the coconut growing states, there is vast scope for increasing the productivity levels. Only area effect has contributed maximum to the increased production observed during the last forty years. The contribution of productivity effect is of very small magnitude. It is also obvious that the performance of Kerala has greater bearing on the all India production. It is also observed that the present productivity level in India is lower than the productivity of the late fifties. This declining trend could be attributed to the low productivity in Kerala due to the spread of the debilitating root disease and frequent occurrence of drought. In the root affected areas, removal of senile, unproductive and diseased palms, planting high yielding and tolerant varieties and better management practices can go a long way in reversing the declining trend in productivity. In the northern districts of Kerala where dry spell extends to 5-6 months, irrigation during the dry period will be advantageous. Further there is greater scope for expansion of area in the states other than Kerala and in the non-traditional areas.

TRENDS IN AREA, PRODUCTION AND PRODUCTIVITY IN KARNATAKA

In India coconut development was brought within the purview of National Plan from 1955-56 onwards. Since then, as a result of the intensive efforts of the erstwhile Indian Central Coconut Committee in association with the Governments of the major coconut growing states, substantial progress could be made in achieving a breakthrough in the expansion of area under the crop. However, after the committee was wound up in 1966, the momentum of the efforts made could last only for another four or five years and thereafter no perceptible improvements could become manifest in the expansion of area in any of the major coconut growing states. The situation is slowly improving, since the Coconut Development Board has taken up area expansion programmes on a priority basis since 1982-83. The following table gives the details of the area under cultivation and production of coconut from 1980 to 1994 in Karnataka.

It can be observed from the above table that there is considerable improvement in area expansion as well as in production of coconut in Karnataka State. It was 171.5 thousand hectares in 1980 and it reached 259 hectares in 1994 with corresponding increase in production of coconut from 890 million nuts (1980) to 1346 million nuts (1994) registering an increase of 33.8 percent in area and 33.9 percent in production. Similarly the yield per hectare was 5190 nuts in 1980 and increased only marginally to 5196 nuts per hectare in 1994 registering an increase of 0.12 percent.

Table 3.7 : Area, Production and Productivity of Coconut in Karnataka

Year	Area (in'000 hectares)	Production (in million nuts	Productivity (in nuts per hectare]
1980	171.5	890.0	5190
1981	172.0	893.2	5193
1982	176.0	914.0	5193
1983	183.0	944.2	5160
1984	193.0	997.0	5165
1985	205.6	1062.0	5165
1986	205.9	1064.0	5168
1987	207.0	1066.0	5150
1988	213.0	1096.0	5146
1989	225.4	1158.0	5141
1990	226.0	1201.6	5317
1991	238.2	1225.3	5143
1992	238.6	1227.6	5145
1993	252.0	1308.0	5190
1994	259.0	1346.0	5196
Compound Growth rate 'r' (in percent)	3.06	3.13	0.01

Source: Karnataka At a Glance, 1994-95, Directorate of Economics and Statistics, Bangalore, 1995.

Compound growth rates of area, production and productivity at the Karnataka State level are estimated to be 3.06, 3.13 and 0.01 percent respectively for the period 1980-81 to 1994-95. The growth rate of productivity at the state level is found to be almost negligible.

TRENDS IN AREA, PRODUCTION AND PRODUCTIVITY OF COCONUT IN TUMKUR DISTRICT

It is a matter of pride to own coconut plantation particularly in Tumkur district. As pointed out earlier that Tumkur is the largest coconut producing district in the state of Karnataka. In terms of contribution to the total area, production in the state, it accounted for 23.94 percent and 36.02 percent respectively in 1994-95,

Tumkur is one of the largest producers of coconut in the state with the total output 432 million nuts in 1994-95.

The importance attached to this crop can be known by analyzing the area under coconut, the quantum of production and productivity.

Table 3.8 : Area, Production and Productivity of Coconut in Tumkur District

Year	Area (in'000 hectares)	Production (in million nuts	Productivity (in nuts per hectare]
1984	47.0	270.0	5574
1985	50.0	278.1	5562
1986	54.1	360.0	6650
1987	51.1	340.0	6645
1988	51.5	342.2	6645
1989	53.0	352.3	6647
1990	54.0	359.0	6645
1991	54.0	359.0	6646
1992	55.2	369.0	6646
1993	59.0	392.1	6646
1994	62.0	412.2	6649
1995	65.0	432.0	6646
Compound Growth rate r' (in percent)	2.35	3.51	1.25

Source: Karnataka At a Glance, 1994-95, District Statistical Office, Tumkur, 1995.

A keen observation of the Table 3.08 shows that both area and production of coconut in Tumkur are showing steady growth with an increasing trend. However, the average yield per hectare has remained almost constant with little variation in between the years.

The area under coconut cultivation has increased from 47.0 thousand hectares in 1983-84 to 65.0 thousand hectares in 1994-95 recording an increase of 27.69 percent. Correspondingly the production has also increased from 270 million nuts in 1983-84 to 432 million nuts in 1994-95 recording an increase of 37.5 percent. The increase in area cultivated and production are moving simultaneously with increasing trend. The year 1991-92 was a period of boom for coconut farmers as they could obtain highly remunerative prices for their produce. The increase in price was almost 100 percent over the previous year. But the prices slumped a little during the years after 1992 with sharp fluctuation.

Compound growth rates of area production and productivity at the Tumkur District level are estimated to be 2.35, 3.51 and 1.25 percent respectively for the period 1984-85 to 1995-96. As compared to the growth rates at all India and Karnataka levels, the performance of Tumkur district is found to be far better. However the growth rate of productivity in the Tumkur district is not found to be satisfactory.

Table 3.9 : Area Under Coconut in Major Coconut Growing Districts in Karnataka

(in '000 hectares)

Year	Tumkur	Hassan	Chitra-durga	Chikma-galur	Others	Total
1980	25.0	34.0	20.0	20.0	72.5	171.5
1981	26.4	34.0	22.4	20.0	102.8	172.0
1982	30.1	36.1	24.0	20.0	65.8	176.0
1983	34.0	38.0	25.4	20.4	65.2	183.0
1984	47.0	38.1	26.4	24.0	57.5	193.0
1985	50.0	38.1	28.0	24.3	65.2	205.6
1986	54.1	38.2	27.5	24.5	61.6	205.9
1987	51.1	41.2	28.1	25.0	61.6	207.0
1988	51.5	42.0	30.0	25.0	64.5	213.0
1989	53.0	42.0	32.0	25.0	73.4	225.4
1990	54.0	42.0	34.3	25.0	70.7	226.0
1991	54.0	42.0	35.0	25.0	82.2	238.2
1992	55.2	42.5	36.2	25.3	79.4	238.6
1993	59.0	44.0	36.3	25.4	87.3	252.0
Compound Growth rate 'r' (in per cent)	6.44	1.93	4.95	2.09	0.74	3.06

Source: Karnataka At a Glance, 1993-94, Bureau of Economics and Statistics. Bangalore, 1994.

Table 3.10: Production of Coconut in Major Coconut Growing Districts in Karnataka

(in million nuts)

Year	Tumkur	Hassan	Chitra-durga	Chikma-galur	Others	Total
1980	88.1	187.0	120.1	50.1	444.7	890.0
1981	96.0	189.0	133.1	51.1	424.0	893.2
1982	106.7	201.8	139.5	50.1	415.9	914.0
1983	120.4	211.0	150.3	51.9	410.6	944.2
1984	270.0	213.0	156.3	60.8	296.9	997.0
1985	278.0	213.0	163.0	62.0	346.0	1062.0
1986	360.0	213.6	162.3	62.4	265.8	1064.0
1987	340.0	230.1	166.0	62.4	267.5	1066.0
1988	342.2	233.4	175.2	63.0	282.2	1096.0
1989	352.3	234.0	189.0	63.1	320.3	1158.7
1990	359.0	234.5	203.0	63.4	341.7	1201.6
1991	359.0	235.0	207.0	63.4	360.9	1225.3
1992	369.0	237.4	214.0	65.0	342.2	1227.6
1993	392.1	244.5	215.0	65.0	121.4	1308.0
Compound Growth rate 'r' (in per cent)	12.77	1.98	4.28	2.16	-4.72	3.06

Source: Karnataka At a Glance, 1993-94, Bureau of Economics and Statistics, Bangalore, 1994.

Table 3.11: Productivity of Coconut in Major Coconut Growing Districts in Karnataka

(in nuts pre hectare)

Year	Tumkur	Hassan	Chitra-durga	Chikma-galur	Others	Total
1980	3537	5582	5917	2592	5190	
1981	3619	5607	5925	2573	5193	
1982	3544	5584	5901	2532	5193	
1983	3566	5591	5914	2545	5160	
1984	5574	5594	5913	2550	5165	
1985	5562	5590	5910	2543	5165	
1986	6650	5592	5912	2546	5168	
1987	6645	5592	5912	2546	5150	
1988	6645	5591	5912	2545	5146	
1989	6647	5592	5911	2546	5141	
1990	6645	5591	5912	2546	5317	
1991	6646	5592	5912	2546	5143	
1992	6646	5592	5912	2546	5145	
1993	6646	5592	5912	2546	5190	
Compound Growth rate 'r' (in per cent)	5.95	9.75	-0.01	-0.07	-4.17	

Source: Karnataka At a Glance, 1993-94, Bureau of Economics and Statistics, Bangalore, 1994.

There are 19 districts in the State and almost all the district cultivate coconut. But the sample district chosen for our study has a unique place in the layout, with maximum coverage of area, production as well as high yield rate. The tables 3.9, 3.10 and 3.11 give the details of area, production and productivity of major coconut growing of districts in Karnataka.

Considering districtwise area, production and productivity of coconut in Karnataka during 1980-81, Hassan district was found to be dominant in areawise, Chitradurga district dominant in productionwise. But drastic change could be seen in the area, production and yield after 1985. Tumkur district out did other districts. For instance during 1989-90 the area under coconut cultivation was 53 thousand hectares (Table 3.9) and the production stood at 352.3 million nuts (Table 3.10) with an yield rate of 6647 per hectare (Table 3.11). And this trend has continued thereafter.

Compound growth rates of area in case of major coconut growing districts like Tumkur, Hassan, Chitradurga and Chikmagalore are estimated to be 6.44, 1.93, 4.95 and 2.09 percent respectively for the period 1980-81 to 1993-94.

Compound growth rates of production in case of major coconut growing districts like Tumkur, Hassan, Chitradurga and Chikmagalore are estimated to be 12.77, 1.98, 4.28 and 2.16 percent respectively for the period 1980-81 to 1993-94.

Compound growth rates of productivity in the above mentioned districts estimated to be 5.95, 9.75 and -0.01 and -0.07 percent respectively for the period 1980-81 to 1993-94. The growth rates in Chitradurga and Chikmagalore districts are found to be negative.

It could be interesting to note the growth trends in area cultivated, production and productivity at National, State and District levels. This helps us to know the contribution of Tumkur district in terms of area, production and productivity to the State and the National level. This is obtained from the Table 3.12.

Table 3.12: Trends in Area, Production and Productivity (yield) at National, State and Tumkur District levels.

Year		India	Karnataka	Tumkur
1985-86				
Area	(A)	1226.00	205.6	50.0
Production	(P)	6770.3	1062.0	278.1
Yield	(Y)	5524.0	5165.0	5562.0
1989-90				
Area	(A)	1490.0	225.4	53.0
Production	(P)	8229.3	1158.7	352.3
Yield	(Y)	5524.0	5141.0	6647.0
1994-95				
Area	(A)	1897.0	259.0	62.0
Production	(P)	10479.0	1346.0	412.2
Yield	(Y)	5524.0	5196.0	6649.0
Percentage change				
in 1994-95	(A)	54.73	25.97	24.00
Over	(P)	54.78	26.74	48.22
1985-86	(Y)	NIL	0.60	19.54

It is observed from the Table 3.12 that the area expansion under coconut at the National level has shown better performance than the State and district levels. At the national level the area under coconut has increased by 54.73 percent in 1994-95 over the base year 1985-86. At the State and Tumkur district levels, the area under coconut has increased by 25.97 percent and 24 percent respectively in 1994-95 over the base year 1985-86. At the National level and district level, production has increased by 54.78 percent and 48.22 percent in 1994-95 over the base year 1985-86 respectively. At the State level production has increased by only 26.74 percent during the above period. However, it is the Tumkur district which has excelled the National and State level performance in terms of productivity. The productivity has increased by 19.54 percent in Tumkur district whereas at the State level, the productivity has increased by only 0.6 percent and at the National level, productivity has remained stagnant and no change has been taken place in the productivity.

It can ultimately be inferred that the position of Tumkur district in the coconut economy in terms area, production and productivity is far better than that of the State and the National levels. This shows the importance of coconut plantation in Tumkur district.

ESTABLISHMENT OF THE COCONUT DEVELOPMENT BOARD

Sensing the need for revamping the situation the Central Government, by an act of parliament constituted the Coconut Development Board in 1981 for the integrated development of coconut industry in the country. Till then the coconut development activities were mainly confined to production and distribution of planting material by maintaining coconut nurseries and seed gardens in state sectors. The development programmes were implemented as centrally sponsored schemes and that too mainly in the states of Kerala, Karnataka, Tamil Nadu, Andhra Pradesh, Orissa etc. Apart from the production of planting materials thrusts were given to the package of practices also. However, these measures were not adequate to the expected level of development. With the formation of the Board, the development programmes for coconut were given a new dimension by identifying key area in which efforts were to be concentrated. The first and foremost objective was to create a sizable future production potential and this objective could be achieved only by stepping up area under coconut systematically over a period of years. Hence, expansion of area under coconut in suitable belts was given top priority as a major component in the development programmes of Board.

The product diversification and by-product utilization in the post harvest processing sector were not given adequate priority till the formation of the Board. The only processing activities carried out were the traditional copra making and oil milling. As such, the coconut industry survived only on coconut oil which is subject to fluctuation very often. The Board, therefore, developed a stringent strategy for coconut development in the country. The core components of the strategy were production of planting materials of improved varieties and hybrids, productivity improvement in the traditional belts, expansion of area in favourable locations and technology development for product diversification and by-product utilisation.

VI AND VII PLAN PROGRAMMES

In the VI and VII plan programmes emphasis was mainly given on eradication of root will affected palms in Kerala and Tamil Nadu, strengthening of existing coconut nurseries of various state departments, expansion of area under coconut etc. Establishment of D.S.P. farms (Demonstration cum Seed Production farm) were initiated during the seventh plan period to ensure supply of quality planting materials. Productivity improvement programmes were formulated to be implemented in root wilt disease affected belts by promoting the two basic requirements identified for productivity improvement viz., promotion of irrigation and a regular system of cutting and removal of diseased/ senile palms and replanting with quality seedlings along with adequate organic recycling process. Irrigation was given major thrust not only for improving productivity but also to increase the net income and employment through adoption of multiple cropping pattern. In the disease free belts and in other states major thrusts were given on area expansion and irrigation by providing incentive subsidy to farmers to boost up the interest of the farmers in taking up coconut cultivation.

Production and quality planting material was given priority by establishing demonstration- cum seed production farms in suitable belts preferably in non-traditional areas. Above all, research and development support was provided for product diversification and by-product utilization. Implementation of these development programmes altogether resulted in a conspicuous change and overall increase in the crop area, production and productivity in the 1980's.

The area under crop increased from the level of 0.8 to 1 million hectares in 1980-81 to the level of 1 to 5 million hectares in 1990-91 registering an increase of 2 to 4 lakh hectares during the decade. The pace of increase was much faster during the second half i.e. 1985 to 90, commencing with seventh plan period when the Board's programmes were implemented on full swing. During this plan period an area of 3 lakh hectares was newly brought under coconut. Major coconut growing states in Kerala, Tamil Nadu, Karnataka and Andhra Pradesh have contributed substantially for the increase in area. Besides, the crop was introduced in several non-traditional belts like Bihar, Madhya Pradesh and North Eastern region. As regards the production the achievement recorded in the decade 1980-90 was higher than that was achieved during three decades between 1950 and 1980. The growth rate during the VII plan period in the case of area was 5 percent and that for production was 6 percent and the productivity registered a revival from stagnation. A major policy decision was also taken by the Govt. of India in 1990 by declaring the crop as an oilseed of tree crop origin.

VIII PLAN PROGRAMMES

VIII plan programmes were formulated keeping in view of the projected demand of 15 million nuts by the end of the plan period and also to find out various end uses of coconut, so as to make use of the additional production potential. The majority of the development programmes undertaken by the Coconut Development Board since its inception in 1981 have been implemented through the State Governments.

The major thrust areas identified for promoting coconut culture and industry in the country during the 8th plan period were:

1. To step up the production of quality planting material.
2. To create future production potential by bringing more area under coconut.
3. Integrated productivity of coconut.
4. Improving control of major pets and diseases.
5. Technology development for product diversification and by-product utilization.

Collection and compilation of basic data on the techno-economic aspects of coconut industry, extension activities for dissemination of information and transfer of technology to the farming community and market promotion of coconut products are the other development programmes of the Board for the balanced development of the coconut industry.

To accomplish the desired objectives, the following programmes have been formulated for implementation during the plan period.

1. The production and distribution of quality planting material.
2. Expansion of area under coconut.
3. Integrated farming in coconut holdings for productivity improvement.
4. Integrated control of leaf eating cater pillar.
5. Establishment of a coconut technology development centre.
6. Extension and publication activities.
7. Establishment of National information and Documentation Centre for Coconut.

1. Production and Distribution of Planting Materials

The objective of the project is to enhance the production and supply of quality planting material. The essential components of the project are the following:

(a) Establishment of Demonstration-cum-Seed Production (DSP) farms

Five Demonstration-cum-seed production farms for coconut have been established in the states of Karnataka, Bihar, Madhya Pradesh, Assam and Tripura. The objective of the programmes is to produce genetically superior planting material and to demonstrate to the farmers the scientific methods of coconut culture in addition to creating a permanent source of income to the Board. The farm established at Mandya (Karnataka) is in the productive stage. In addition, 5 more farms, in Kerala (2 farms of 20 ha each), Karnataka (20 ha) Andhra Pradesh (40 ha) and Orissa (40 ha) were established during the VIII plan period. The programme was operated directly by the Board and the budget estimate for the plan period was Rs. 367.9 lakhs.

(b) Establishment of Coconut Nurseries attached to DSP Farms

Quality seedlings with target of 3 lakhs of improved local varieties were being produced and distributed annually by the Demonstration-cum-seed production Farms of the Board established at Mandya (Karnataka), Madhepura (Bihar), Abhayapuri (Assam) and Neriamangalm (Kerala). The total outlay earmarked for the plan period was Rs. 208.478 lakhs. The programme was directly implemented by the Board.

(c) Establishment of Regional Coconut Nurseries

In order to meet the existing demand for quality planting material it was proposed to supplement the nursery programme by extending financial assistance for establishing Regional Coconut Nurseries in Nagaland and Union Territory of Lakshadweep. The scheme was implemented through the respective Governments of the State/Union Territory. It is envisaged to produce and distribute 20,000 seedlings annually from each unit with a total financial outlay of Rs. 22.8 lakhs of which the share of the Board would be Rs. 17.1 lakhs.

(d) Establishment of a seed procurement unit attached to the headquarters of the Board

The objective is to assist different State Governments and other agencies in the procurement and supply of quality seed nuts. Seed coconuts are procured form reputed disease free location from selected mother palms and supply to indenting agencies. This is a continuing programme. The target fixed under the programme is to procure and supply 5 lakhs seed nuts annually. The total financial outlay for the programmes on establishment was Rs. 12 lakhs which could be fully met by the Board.

(e) Production and Distribution of TXD Hybrid Coconut seedlings

This is a continuing programme, the objective of which is to improve the genetic potential of coconut in the country through the production and distribution of Tall x Dwarf hybrids required for regular planting in the potential belts. The programme has been continued in the states of Kerala, Tmail Nadu, Andhra Pradesh, Orissa, Mahashtra and in the Union Territory of Lakshadweep Island. The annual production target is 1,50,000 seeldings for Kerala, 1,00,000 each for Tamil Nadu and Andhra Pradesh, 50,000 for Orissa and 25,000 each for Maharashtra and Lakshadweep. The estimated expenditure was Rs. 394.992 lakhs for the plan period of which the Board's share for the programme was Rs. 207.090 lakhs.

2. Expansion of Area under coconut

Considerable extent of land suitable for coconut culture is available in both the traditional and non-traditional coconut belts in the country. Adequate technical and financial support should be given to the farmers to attain a significant achievement in expanding the area under coconut.

With this objective in view the Coconut Development Board has been implementing a programme since 1982-83 for expanding the area under coconut. The programme has continued during the plan period by providing a subsidy of Rs. 6,000 per ha to be disbursed in three annual instalments. It was proposed to cover a physical target of 24900 ha covering all the coconut growing States/Union Territories. It was also proposed to introduce the crop in suitable non-traditional belts. The total financial outlay for the programme during the plan period was Rs. 1556.66 lakhs. The programme has been implemented by the Board in close collaboration with the Agriculture/Horticulture Department of the States/UTs concerned.

3. Integrated Farming in Coconut Holdings for Productivity Improvement

This is the major productivity improvement programme being implement in Kerala, Tamil Nadu, Karnataka, Andhra Pradesh, Maharashtra, Pondicherry, Andaman Nicobar Islands, Goa and Lakshadweep Islands during the plan period.

The main objective of the programme is to improve

production and productivity of the crop through an integrated approach. Technical contents of the programme were to cut and remove the disease affected and senile palms, replanting with quality seedlings wherever optimum planting density does not exceed, improve the management practices like fertilizer applications, adoption of plant protection measures and multi species cropping etc. The programme covered

1. Removal of disease advanced/ senile palms by paying compensation at the rate of Rs. 200 per palm.
2. Replanting with quality seedlings preferably hybrids to maintain an optimum plant population per unit area with a subsidy of Rs. 5 per seedling.
3. Subsidised supply of fertilizer application for coconut and plant protection measures at the rate of Rs. 8 per palm.
4. Growing multispecies crop combination in the coconut holdings including green manure crops with a grant of Rs. 200 per ha towards the cost of planting materials.

The total operational area for the programme was 100,000 ha for Kerala, 10,000 ha each for Karnataka and Tamil Nadu, 14,000 ha for Andhra Pradesh, 200 ha each for Maharashtra and Goa and 800 ha each for Pondicherry, Lakshadweep and Andaman and Nicobar Islands, thus bringing the total operational area to 1,36,800 ha during the plan period.

The total cost of the project for the plan period was Rs. 3345 lakhs which was fully met by the Board. The programme has been implemented by the respective State Governments in collaboration with the Coconut Development Board.

4. Integrated Coconut of Leaf Eating Caterpillar

With a view to controlling the prevalence of the serious pets and the black headed caterpillar, a programme of integrated control was envisaged by establishing 4 new biological control laboratory units, one each in Karnataka, Andhra Pradesh, Tamil Nadu and Kerala. The units are meant for cultivating multiplying and maintaining parasites for release in pest prone area and for implementing other plant protection measures. These units are in addition to the already established units in Karnataka and Orissa. The total cost of the project was Rs. 78.065 lakhs of which the share of the Board was Rs. 46.481 lakhs.

The outlays for the various programmes of Coconut Development Board for the VIII plan period (1992-97) and the allocations for development of coconut cultivation under various plan periods are given in the Table 3.12 and Table 3.13 respectively.

5. Technology Development for Product Diversification and By-Product Utilisation

The projected demand for coconut at the end of the plan period is 15 billion nuts as against present supply of 10 billion nuts. The development programmes are formulated in such a way as to bridge the gap between the demand and supply. With the implementation of the development programmes of the Board the crop area would also increase to the level of 2 million hectares as against the present area of 1.5 million hectares under coconut. About 3 million seedlings would be made available for meeting the increasing demand for coconut seedlings both in traditional as well as non-traditional belts. It is intended to introduce the crop in suitable non-traditional belts like Uttar Pradesh, Rajasthan, Meghalaya, Arunachal Pradesh, Mizoram, Chandigarh, Dadra and Nagar Havelo, Daman and Diu etc. In addition efforts are being made to save foreign exchange to the tune of $ 480 million. Additional employment generation expected is 200 million mandays and the number of farm families benefited would be about 3 million. Apart from these, an array of new value added coconut products would be developed with the availability of new technologies and increased production. Coir production for domestic and export markets is expected to rise with the increase in supply of coconut husk, the raw material for coir industry. This would result in increased export earnings and create additional employment opportunities in this sector.

Table 3.13 : Outlay for the Coconut Development Board Programmes for the VIII Plan Preod

(Rs. in lakhs)

Sl. No.	Name of Scheme	Boards share	State share	Total
1.	Production and distribution of planting material			
	(a) EsH. of DSP farms	367.900	-	367.900
	(b) Nursery attached to the DSP farms	208.478	-	208.478
	(c) EsH. of Regional Coconut Nurseries	17.100	5.7000	22.8000
	(d) Seed procurement Unit	12.000	-	12.000
	(e) TXD scheme	207.900	187.902	394.992
	(f) EsH. of 100 ha hybrid seed garden	4.9000	4.9000	9.800
2.	Expansion of area under coconut	1566.660	-	1556.660
3.	Integrated fareming in coconut holdings	3345.000	120.000	3465.000
4.	Irrigation scheme	91.858	13.158	105.016
5.	Integrated control of leaf eating caterpillar	46.481	31.584	78.065
6.	Technology development Centre	572.800	-	572.800
7.	Publicity and Extension activity	356.100	-	356.100
8.	National Information and Documentation centre for coconut	41.556	-	41.556
9.	Infrastructure and administration	1101.077	-	1101.077
	Total	7929.000	363.244	8292.244

Source: Government of Karnataka, Draft VIII Plan (1992-97), Planning Department, December, 1991.

Table 3.14 : Allocations for Coconut Development Under Different Plans

(Rs. in lakhs)

Plan	Year	Board's share	State share	Total
Sixth	1980-85	538.00	409.00	947.00
Seventh	1985-90	1080.00	314.00	1384.00
Annual	1990-91	257.00	30.25	287.25
Annual	1991-92	560.00	101.10	661.10
Eighth	1992-97	7929.00	363.244	8292.244

Source: (1) Govt. of India, Draft Sixth Five Year Plan Vol.11.

(2) Govt. of India, Seventh Five Year Plan

(3) Govt. of India, Eighth Five Year Plan.

Consumption pattern of coconut and coconut products are undergoing vast changes. Demand for tender nuts especially in the large metropolitan cities goes on increasing at a faster pace. This is mainly because of the emerging shift in taste of the people from artificial soft drinks to natural drinks. In Kerala State which accounts for 50 percent of the production of coconut, the tender nut trade was comparatively absent. But recently retail trade in tender nut has been picking up in all the major towns. Among the food uses of coconut, demand for mature nuts and desiccated coconut even in the non-traditional areas is registering an accelerated increase. Besides household edible uses is mature nut is in demand as an essential item in social, cultural and religious functions. Around 60 percent of the total production is utilised for this purpose. The demand for edible and non edible uses of coconut is likely to grow fast. The requirement of coconut for seed purposes is on the increase in view of the expansion of area under the crop in traditional and non-traditional regions. The present demand is around 20 million nuts for seed purpose alone. The present production of coconut oil is around 3 lakh tonnes. Coconut oil is used for edible and non-edible purposes. The consumption of coconut oil for edible uses is around 40 percent of the production. Taking into account the existing demand as well as the future uses of coconut and coconut products, it is estimated that the rate of growth of demand for coconut and coconut products was around 8 percent during the VIII plan period and is likely grow at 10 percent thereafter upto 2000 A.D.[6] Coconut by-products such as husk and shell are in great need especially for export oriented by-products. The demand for shell is likely to grow at a faster pace especially to meet the demand from western countries for natural containers and shell based activated carbon. In addition, agro processing sector based on fresh kernel would develop in the coming years, as the technology for diversified products like coconut cream, cream power etc. is already or likely to be available for commercial exploitation.

REFERENCES

1. Thampan, P.K. : *Profitable Coconut Growing*, Coconut Development Board, Ministry of Agriculture, Govt. of India, Cochin, Kerala, 1984, pp. 1 - 58.

2. Mandal, R.C.: *Coconut Production and Protection Technology*, Indian Council of Agricultural Research, Krishi Bhavan, 1991, pp. 1 - 168.
3. Central Plantation Crops Research Institute: Coconut Root (Wilt) Disease: A survey report, CPCRI, Kasaragod, 1985, p 15.
4. George, M.V.: Thommen, K.J. and Sukumaran, A.S.: *Incidence of Root (Wilt) and Leaf-rot Diseased and Oryetes Infestation Symposium Plantation Crops* (Ed) Venkataraman C.S. pp. 27 - 28.
5. Thampan, P.K.: *Glimpses of Coconut Industry in India*, Edited by Muhammed Edchal and T.B. Nandakumar. Coconut Development Board, Cochin, 1988, p. 219.
6. Markose, V.T.: *Coconut Development in the Lost Decade*, Indian Coconut Journal, Vol. XXV, No.7, 1994, p. 12.

CHAPTER 4

COST OF CULTIVATION

In this Chapter, a brief socio-economic profile of sample farmers is presented first. Then an attempt has been made to estimate the cost of cultivation of coconut plantation with the help of information provided by the sample farmers in both irrigated and unirrigated areas.

SOCIO-ECONOMIC PROFILE OF SAMPLE FARMERS

Some of the important features of the sample farmers such as family size, level of education, area under coconut and other crops etc. have been presented here.

Family Size

The sample farmers are presented according to the size of family in the Table 4.1. It could be observed from the table that the number of families with members between (6-10) was arge. There were 54 families in this size group constituting about 45 percent of the total number of families. This is followed by the size group (1-5) with 32 families accounting for 26.67 percent of the total. 23.33 percent of

Table 4.1 : Distribution of Farmers According to Family Size

Sl. No.	Family Size (No. of Members)	No. of families in Size Group			Total No. of Families
		Small	Medium	Large	
1.	1-5	20	10	2	32 (26.67)
2.	6-10	18	16	20	54 (45.00)
3.	11-15	2	14	12	28 (23.33)
4.	16-20	-	-	6	6 (5.00)
	Total				120 (100)

Source: Field Survey.

N.B. : Figures in parentheses indicate percentage to the total.

the farmers belonged to the size group (11-15) members. Of the total number of families in all the three size-groups, the family size (6-10) was the popular and this was followed by the family size (1-5). The average family size of the sample farmers is worked to be 8.33.

Education

The adoption of improved methods of agriculture such as use of agricultural machinery, application of fertilizer etc., requires on the part of the farmers certain level of education and training. So the sample farmers have been distributed on the basis of their education in the Table 4.2.

Table 4.2: Distribution of Sample Farmers According to Education

Sl. No.	Category	Small	Medium	Large	Total
1.	Illiterate farmer	12	15	10	37
2.	Upto lower primary	8	9	8	25
3.	Above lower primary and upto higher primary	8	5	10	23
4.	Above higher primary and upto S.S.L.C.	9	4	2	15
5.	Pre-University	2	3	4	9
6.	Graduation	1	4	6	11
	Total	40	40	40	120

Source: Field Survey.
N.B. : Figures in parentheses indicate percentage to the total.

The number of illiterate farmers was 37 forming about 30.83 percent of the total. There were 25 farmes (20.83 percent of the total) with education upto lower primary, 23 farmers (19.17 percent) with education above lower primary and upto higher primary, 15 farmers (12.5 percent) had passed S.S.L.C., 9 farmers (7.5 percent) had passed PUC and 11 farmers (9.17) had passed graduate degree examination. There was no farmer with basic training in agricultural sciences.

AREA UNDER COCONUT AND OTHER CROPS

The total gross cropped area of the sample farmers was 903.11 acres. Coconut was the predominant crop occupying an area of 579.26 acres forming 64.14 percent of the gross cropped area. Area under all other crops together occupied an area of 323.85 acres forming 35.86 percent of the gross cropped area.

It is clear from the Table 4.3 that the percentage of area under coconut to the gross cropped area in case of large and medium farmers was relatively more as compared to that of small farmers. The reason for this is that large and medium farmers want to be make large profits by bringing more land under coconut and are ready to face risk involved in the cultivation of coconut palms.

Table 4.3: Area Under Coconut and Other Crops Grown by the Sample Farmers

Sl. No.	Crops	Size Group						Total
		Irrigated			Unirrigated			
		Small	Medium	Large	Small	Medium	Large	
1.	Coconut	48.03 (08.29)	130.35 (22.50)	248 (42.81)	29.78 (05.14)	47.10 (08.13)	76.00 (13.12)	579.26 (100.00)
2.	Other crops	23.5 (07.26)	36.25 (11.19)	63.10 (19.48)	20.05 (06.19)	54.75 (16.91)	126.2 (38.97)	323.85 (100.00)
	Gross Cropped	71.53 (07.92)	166.6 (18.45)	311.1 (34.45)	49.83 (05.52)	101.85 (11.28)	202.2 (22.39)	903.11

Source: Field Survey.

N.B. : Figures in parentheses indicate percentage to the gross cropped area.

COST OF CULTIVATION OF COCONUT

Any useful study on the economics of coconut should include an effective cost analysis. A discussion on the cost analysis will help us in knowing the investment in bringing up a coconut garden and the expenditure for maintaining such a garden, Coconut is a plantation crop and the farmer will have to wait at least for a period of 6 to 7 years for the yield. As a result, the farmer has no other option than to invest without having any benefits during this period. Further a coconut tree will have a life span exceeding 50 to 60 years[1]. For proper maintenance of the coconut plantations and for improving the yields, the farmer has to sent out large amounts of money. There is a general apprehension about the cost involved, the returns or profitability of having a coconut plantation.

In this section an attempt is made to estimate the various kinds of expenditure incurred by the coconut farmers for

Table 4.4: Per Acre Cost of Cultivation of Coconut in Case of Small Farmers (Irrigated), 1994-95

(Qty in numbers) (Values in Rs.)

ITEMS OF EXPENDITURE	Year of Establishment Period														Total	Economic Period	
	I		II		III		IV		V		VI		VII			VIII	
	Qty	Val	Qty	Val	Qty	Val	Qty	Val	Qty	Val	Qty	Val	Qty	Val		Qty	Val
(A) Material Cost:																	
1. (a) Seedlings @ Rs.30/ seedlings	47	1457	2	62	1	31	-	-	-	-	-	-	-	-	1550	-	-
(b) Supports @ Rs.2.00/ supports	47	94	2	4	1	2	-	-	-	-	-	-	-	-	100	-	-
2. **Compost** (Rs.400/ tractor load)	0.50	200	0.50	200	0.40	180	0.51	204	0.40	160	0.65	260	0.70	280	1484	0.60	240
3. **Fertilizers**																	
Suphala (Rs.5.92/Kg)	10	59	16	95	11	65	22	130	20	118	23	136	25	148	751	24	142
Super Phosphate (Rs.3.02/Kg)	12	36	30	91	15	45	-	-	-	-	-	-	16	48	220	-	-
Muriate of Potash (Rs.3.90/Kg)	-	-	28	32	11	43	-	-	-	-	-	-	12	47	122	-	-
Urea (Rs. 3.40/Kg)	-	-	23	78	20	68	-	-	-	-	-	-	21	82	228	-	-
Neem Cake (Rs.2.50/Kg)	-	-	-	1	3	-	-	-	-	-	-	-	-	-	3	-	-
Read earth (Rs.55/tractor load)	2.50	138	0.75	41	0.5	26	-	-	-	-	-	-	-	-	207	-	-
Sand (Rs.55/tractor load)	1.50	83	-	-	-	-	-	-	-	-	-	-	-	-	83	-	-
Plant protection chemical (B.H.C. Rs. 48/Kg)	0.5	24	1	48	0.75	36	1.10	53	1	48	1.28	61	1	48	318	1	48

[contd...]

Table 4.4: [contd...]

(Qty in numbers) (Values in Rs.)

ITEMS OF EXPENDITURE	Year of Establishment Period															Economic Period	
	I		II		III		IV		V		VI		VII		Total	VIII	
	Qty	Val	Qty	Val	Qty	Val	Qty	Val	Qty	Val	Qty	Val	Qty	Val		Qty	Val
(B) Irrigation Cost:																	
(a) Cost of irrigation (NO.) Rs. 120/irrigation	12	1440	9	1080	10	1200	11	1320	11	1320	10	1200	10	1200	8760	9	1080
(C) Labour Cost:																	
1. (a) Land Preparation (Rs.40/bullock pair per day)	6	240	-	-	-	-	-	-	-	-	-	-	-	-	240	-	-
(b) Levelling (Rs. 40/bullock pair per day)	5	200	-	-	-	-	-	-	-	-	-	-	-	-	200	-	-
(c) Bunding (Rs. 30/mandayas)	10	300	-	-	-	-	-	-	-	-	-	-	-	-	300	-	-
2. Digging Pits (contact at Rs. 8/pit)	47	376	-	-	-	-	-	-	-	-	-	-	-	-	376	-	-
3. Planting (Rs.30/mandays)	6	180	-	-	-	-	-	-	-	-	-	-	-	-	180	-	-
4. Application of compost & fertilizers (Rs. 30/mandays)	3	90	3	90	2	60	2	60	2	60	2	60	3	90	510	2	60
5. Plant protection (Rs. 30/mandays)	2	60	1	30	2	60	2	50	2	60	2	60	2	60	390	1	30

[contd...]

Table 4.4: *[contd...]*

(Qty in numbers) (Values in Rs.)

ITEMS OF EXPENDITURE	Year of Establishment Period														Total	Economic Period	
	I		II		III		IV		V		VI		VII			VIII	
	Qty	Val	Qty	Val	Qty	Val	Qty	Val	Qty	Val	Qty	Val	Qty	Val		Qty	Val
6. Weeding & widening of basins (Rs. 30/mandays)	8	240	4	120	5	150	3	90	4	120	4	120	4	120	960	4	120
7. Irrigating (Rs. 30/mandays)	12	360	10	300	11	330	10	300	11	330	11	330	10	300	2250	9	270
8. Permanent Labour for both watch & ward and harvesting	-	200	-	250	-	250	-	350	-	355	-	355	-	430	2190	-	480
Total of A + B +C	-	5775	-	2521	-	2548	-	2750	-	2571	-	2582	-	2853	21422	-	2470
Interest on amount invested during the previous year (10%)	-	-	-	578	-	252	-	255	-	257	-	257	-	258	285	-	2171
Total cost during the year		5777		3099		2800		2825		2828		2839		3111	21707		4641

Source: Field Survey.

N.B. : Figures in value column are rounded off

brining up and maintaining coconut plantation. Costs involved in the cultivation of a coconut plantation and its maintenance may be divided into two categories. Category one includes fixed costs covering that of land and machinery and amount spent on irrigation and other overheads. The category two is variable costs covering that of labour, fertilizer, land preparation, harvesting etc. On the assumption that there is no fixed cost in the long run, all costs will be variable cost. Here some of the details of expenditures incurred during the first year are discussed. This will give an idea about the various aspects of spending by the farmers in the first year and in the subsequent years nut bearing stage. The life span of a coconut tree can be divided into two parts (i) the establishment period i.e. the no yield stage, (ii) the economic period i.e. the nut bearing stage, though the life span of coconut plant exceeds 60 years[2].

In this study the economic viability of bringing up a coconut garden in Tumkur district is analysed by studying the investment proposition in case of irrigated and unirrigated small, medium and large coconut farmers. Such an analysis on the cost of cultivation is of great importance from the economic point of view to farmers who wish to venture into coconut plantation and also to those financial institutions who wish to extend support to coconut growers.

For arriving at cost and returns estimates, the wage rates and prices prevailing in the study area during the 1994-95 were considered. Wage rate of Rs. 30 per manday, Rs. 40 per bullock pair per day were prevailing during the study period. Unit cost of per kg of Suphala, Super Phosphate, Muratc of potash, Urea, Neemcake and Chemical B.H.C. were found to be Rs. 5.92, Rs. 3.02, Rs. 3.90, Rs.2.50 and Rs. 48 respectively in the study area. The irrigation charges refer to the cost of labour involved irrigating the coconut trees which involves labour in making canals and regulating water to each basin. All farmers under consideration, on an average have 47 trees per acre.

Coconut is a plantation crop and farmers will have to invest and wait at least for a period of 6 to 7 years to get yield. Therefore an amount of 10 percent of the amount invested in the previous year is taken as part of the expenditure in the current year. Thus a 10 percent of amount spent in the first year is taken as part of expenditure in the second year and so on till seventh year. Similarly a 10 percent of the total expenditure in the establishment period is taken as part of expenditure in the eighth year i.e. first year of economic period.

Since coconut is a perennial crop standing on the field quite a number of years, its economics needs to be considered for the different phases of its life period. To start with the economics of coconut cultivation in case of small farmers in the irrigated area may be evaluated. The information on various costs is presented in the Table 4.4.

ESTABLISHMENT PERIOD

The conventional varieties of coconut take about seven years to establish. The cost of cultivation differs during this period. For instance, the cost per acre during the first year is Rs. 5777. This is very high compared to the cost in other six years during the establishment period. The reason for this may be seen from the table.

The costs of seedlings, land preparation, leveling and bunding which have to be under taken during the first year, are required during the first year. After the first year the cost shows declining trend upto the seventh year. The increase in the seventh year is due to the additional expenditure on fertilizer during that year. According to the farmers the fertilizer charges went up during the seventh year as more fertilizers were applied as the seventh year usually considered as the penultimate year before the tree bears nuts. The cost of seedlings per acre was Rs. 1457 in the first year. The cost of seedlings was thus 25.22 percent of the total cost incurred during the first year. The labour charges consisting of planting, land preparation, leveling, bunding and digging pits, permanent labour for both watch and word and harvesting, weeding and widening of basins, plant protection, application of compost and fertilizers were found to be Rs. 1886 per acre. This accounted for 32.65 percent of the total cost during the first year. Manure and fertilizer charges during the first year surprisingly stood at Rs. 295 constituting just 5.11 percent of the total expenditure. Red soil and river sand form two important ingredients while required the pit for planting. The cost for these two items which required only while planting stood at Rs. 224 which worked out to be 3.88 percent of the total expenditure. The irrigation charges of Rs. 1,800 formed about 31.16 percent of the total expenditure. The cost of cultivation during the first year as stated above found to be high compared to the cost in subsequent years. A look at the table will give a clear idea of the cost during the next six years of the establishment period. On an average a small farmer has incurred an expenditure of coconut plantation out of which the amount of Rs. 5777 has been spent during the first year of plantation which formed the highest expenditure. Out of the total expenditure incurred during the establishment period, 26.61 percent was spent during the first year.

Material Cost

Expenditure on fertilizer forms one of the most important part of the cost during the establishment period. Out of total expenditure Rs. 21707 of which the small farmers spent during he establishment period Rs. 2808 was spent on manure and fertilizers. This constituted 12.94 percent of the total cost during the establishment period. However, it should be noted that the sample farmers have spent much less as compared to the farmers in other parts of the country whose expenditure on fertilizers and manures is about 60 percent of the total cost. Among the fertilizers used, Suphala seems to be the most favourable for which the sample farmers spent Rs. 751 for the seventh year period.

Irrigation Cost

Another major expenditure for the farmers is that of providing irrigation as water forms a very important production factor in coconut cultivation. Low productivity can be directly related to low availability of water. Irrigation is expensive for small and medium farmers. The cost of irrigation was found to be Rs. 120 per irrigation of one acre which forms a major part of the total expenditure. On an average, the small farmers spent Rs. 8760 on irrigating one acre of coconut plantation during the seven year establishment period. Further the labour charges for irrigating one acre of land worked out to be Rs. 2250 during the establishment period. Thus, on an average the small farmer spent Rs. 11010 for providing irrigation to one acre of coconut plantation during the 7 years of establishment period. This constituted about 50.75 percent of the total expenditure.

Labour Cost

The requirement of labour goes on diminishing during the establishment period. Table - 4.4 gives details of the labour requirement for one acre irrigated coconut plantation. This does not include requirement of labour for land preparation, leveling and irrigation. This is because land preparation and leveling etc. have been taken separately and cost of labour for irrigation has been added with irrigation charges. The labour requirements for plant protection, weeding and widening of basins, application of compost and fertilizers for the first seven years in the establishment period were found to be Rs. 5010 per acre constituting 23.08 pecent of the total expenditure. Further it should be noted that the most of the small farmers involved in coconut farming utilize the family labour also. The labour cost as worked out above includes such family labour.

ECONOMIC PERIOD

Economic period of the coconut palm is a controversial topic with different farmer differing in their opinion regarding the economic life of the tree. A look at the reveals that in beginning of the economic period i.e. for 8th year, the expenditure or the cost of cultivation works out to be less than that of any year in the establishment period.

Material Cost

On an average a small farmer spent Rs. 382 per acre on compost and Suphala fertilizer during the first year of the economic period. This sudden fall in the expenditure on fertilizer is due to non application of some of the items which were used in the establishment.

Irrigation Cost

Again, the cost of irrigation has also been reduced. In the study area the farmers are of the opinion that the irrigation requirement for coconut trees is mainly during the establishment period and during the economic period the coconut tree can sustain itself even without irrigation. However, irrigation is done by the farmers because regular irrigation can improve the productivity. During the 8th year the expenditure on irrigation was found to be Rs. 1080 per acre which is less than the establishment period.

Labour Cost

Labour cost is also reduced once the plantation reached the economic priod. The total labour expenditure in the 8th year, as can be seen from the table was Rs. 960 per acre which is low as compared the labour cost in any of the year in the establishment period. The main labour expenditure during the economic period is that of harvesting. The coconut tree unlike the other crops needs very little attention once it reaches the economic period.

The total cost in case of small farmer in the irrigated region during the first year of economic period is found to be Rs. 4641 per acre. In the economic period the trend of cost goes on decreasing and the returns goes on increasing. Of the total cost of cultivation of Rs. 4641 per year in the economic period, 8.23 percent was spent on fertilizer 20.69 percent on labour and 23.27 percent on irrigation.

COST OF CULTIVATION IN CASE OF MEDIUM SIZE FARMERS IN IRRIGATED FARMS

The medium size farmers have to spend a large amount of money during the first year like the small size farmers. Cost analysis in this section is also carried out in two periods namely the establishment period and economic period.

ESTABLISHMENT PERIOD

The Table-4.5 reveals that the medium size farmers in the study area spent on an average Rs. 5497 per acre during the first year. This amount is lower than that of the small size farmers. This is mainly due to economics of scale in various operations during establishment period. However, the amount spent by the medium farmer during year is much higher than the amount spent in the subsequent years of the establishment period. Land preparation, ground

Table 4.5: Per Acre Cost of Cultivation of Coconut in Case of Medium Farmers (Irrigated), 1994-95

(Qty in numbers) (Values in Rs.)

ITEMS OF EXPENDITURE	Year of Establishment Period														Total	Economic Period	
	I		II		III		IV		V		VI		VII			VIII	
	Qty	Val	Qty	Val	Qty	Val	Qty	Val	Qty	Val	Qty	Val	Qty	Val		Qty	Val
(A) Material Cost:																	
1. (a) Seedlings @ Rs.30/ seedlings	47	1445	3	92	2	62	-	-	-	-	-	-	-	-	1599	-	-
(b) Supports @ Rs.2.00/ supports	47	94	3	6	2	4	-	-	-	-	-	-	-	-	104	-	-
2. Compost (Rs.390/ tractor load)	0.50	195	0.50	195	0.30	117	0.52	203	0.48	187	0.65	253	0.70	273	1423	0.60	234
3. Fertilizers																	
Suphala (Rs.5.92/Kg)	9.50	56	13.50	80	12	71	20	118	16	95	19	112	10	59	591	20	118
Super Phosphate (Rs.3.02/Kg)	11.25	34	26	89	13	39	-	-	-	-	-	-	14	42	204	-	-
Muriate of Potash (Rs.3.90/Kg)	-	-	20	78	11	43	-	-	-	-	-	-	13	51	172	-	-
Urea (Rs. 3.40/Kg)	-	-	16	54	15	51	-	-	-	-	-	-	16	54	159	-	-
Neem Cake (Rs.2.50/Kg)	-	-	-	-	10	25	-	-	-	-	-	-	-		25	-	-
Read earth (Rs.55/tractor load)	2.25	119	0.50	27	-	-	-	-	-	-	-	-	-	-	196	-	-
Sand	2	106	-	-	-	-	-	-	-	-	-	-	-	-	106		
Plant protection chemical (B.H.C. Rs. 48/Kg)	0.5	24	1.00	48	0.75	37	1.00	48	1.10	53	1	48	1.00	48	305	1.00	48

[contd...]

Table 4.5: [contd...]

(Qty in numbers) (Values in Rs.)

ITEMS OF EXPENDITURE	Year of Establishment Period														Total	Economic Period	
	I		II		III		IV		V		VI		VII			VIII	
	Qty	Val	Qty	Val	Qty	Val	Qty	Val	Qty	Val	Qty	Val	Qty	Val		Qty	Val
(B) Irrigation Cost:																	
(a) Cost of irrigation (NO.) Rs. 120/irrigation	11	1320	9	1080	10	1200	11	1320	11	1320	10	1200	11	1320	8760	8	960
(C) Labour Cost:																	
1. Land Preparation (a) Tractor Service (Rs. 1.50/hour)	1.25	188	-	-	-	-	-	-	-	-	-	-	-	-	188	-	-
(b) Levelling (Rs. 40/bullock pair per day)	5	200	-	-	-	-	-	-	-	-	-	-	-	-	200	-	-
(c) Bunding (Rs. 30/mandayas)	9	270	-	-	-	-	-	-	-	-	-	-	-	-	270	-	-
2. Digging Pits (contact at Rs. 8/pit)	47	376	-	-	-	-	-	-	-	-	-	-	-	-	376	-	-
3. Planting (Rs.30/mandays)	6	180	-	-	-	-	-	-	-	-	-	-	-	-	180	-	-
4. Application of compost & fertilizers (Rs. 30/mandays)	3	90	2	60	2	60	2	60	3	90	3	90	3	90	540	2	60
5. Plant protection (Rs. 30/mandays)	2	60	1	30	2	60	1	30	2	60	2	60	2	60	360	1	30

[contd...]

Table 4.5: *[contd...]*

(Qty in numbers) (Values in Rs.)

ITEMS OF EXPENDITURE	Year of Establishment Period														Total	Economic Period	
	I		II		III		IV		V		VI		VII			VIII	
	Qty	Val	Qty	Val	Qty	Val	Qty	Val	Qty	Val	Qty	Val	Qty	Val		Qty	Val
6. Weeding & widening of basins (Rs. 30/mandays)	7	210	4	120	5	150	4	120	3	90	4	120	5	150	960	4	120
7. Irrigating (Rs. 30/mandays)	11	330	9	270	10	300	11	330	10	300	10	300	11	330	2160	8	240
8. Permanent Labour for both watch & ward and harvesting	-	200	-	245	-	250	-	255	-	300	-	325	-	380	1955	-	450
Total of A + B +C	-	5497	-	2474	-	2468	-	2484	-	2495	-	2509	-	2857	20781	-	2260
Interest on amount invested during the previous year (10%)	-	-	-	550	-	247	-	247	-	248	-	250	-	251	286	-	2107
Total cost during the year		5497		3024		2715		2731		2743		2759		3108	21067		4367

Source: Field Survey.

N.B. : Figures in value column are rounded off

leveling, expenditure on seedling, planting and digging pits, applying red soil and river sand etc. which are special features of the first year are mainly responsible for high expenditure during the first year. When we analyse the cost in the first year, it is clear that the usual three major items, compost and fertilizer, irrigation and labour cost have the lion share in the total cost. Of the total cost in the first year, Rs. 1650 per acre (30.02 percent) was spent on irrigation.

The cost of labour in the first year for the medium size farmers is amounted to Rs. 1386 per acre. The amount of money spent on the labour forms 25.21 percent of the total cost incurred during the first year.

The cost on fertilizer followed the general trend in the study area. The farmers here believe that application of more fertilizers in the first year have a harmful effect on the coconut plant. The expenditure on fertilizers during the first year in case of medium size farmers is amounted to just Rs. 90 per acre. However, it may be noted that during the subsequent years of the establishment period the expenditure increased and reached the peak in the seventh year. The farmers in the area are very apprehensive about the role of chemical fertilizers.

During the first seven years or the establishment period, the coconut farmers have to spend large amount of money without getting any benefits. Also coconut being a perennial crop with long gestation period, farmers with lesser income are sceptical about the returns. The medium size farmers in the study area as can be seen from the Table -4.5, spent a total of Rs. 21067 during the establishment period.

Material Cost

Fertilizers and manures formed a major part of the expenditure of the medium size farmers. Among the fertilizers and manures applied for the plantation, the cost of compost stood at the highest followed by Suphala. The amount spent on compost was Rs. 1423 per acre and that of Suphala was Rs. 591. The total expenditure on compost and fertilizers stood at Rs. 2575 per acre. The cost of compost formed 55.26 percent of the expenditure on fertilizers and manures. The expenditure on Suphala formed 22.95 percent of the total expenditure. The expenditure on these two items thus crossed the 70 percent mark of total the expenditure on fertilizers. As in the case of small size farmers, the medium size farmers also applied higher doses of fertilizers during the seventh year.

Irrigation Cost

Irrigation cost during the establishment period shows that the total amount spent on irrigation during this period was Rs. 10920 per acre. This amount formed 52.83 percent of the total expenditure incurred during the first seven years. The farmers in the Tumkur area are found to be ignorant about the various soil moisture conservation techniques. Irrigation cost varied from year to year in the establishment period. The yearly expenditure on irrigation on an average worked out to be Rs. 1251 per acre during the establishment period. The irrigation requirement during the establishment period consumed 72 man hours and the total cost for labour involvement during this period amounted to Rs. 2160 per acre.

Labour Cost

The Table-4.5 reveals that the total expenditure on labour for the medium size farmers was Rs. 4641 per acre during the establishment period. Of the various activities, labour used in the application of compost manure took a good number of man hour. The total man hours required for this purpose was 18. The total cost involved in this activity is worked out to be Rs. 540 per acre. The number of man hours used on weeding and widening of basins took 32 man hours. This is the activity for which highest amount of money has been spent. A total of Rs. 960 per acre was spent for this purpose. On an average medium size farmers spent Rs. 6801 per acre accounting for 32.28 percent of the total expenditure incurred during the establishment period.

ECONOMIC PERIOD

Material Cost

In case of medium size farmers, the average expenditure on fertilizers during the 8th year i.e. the first year of economic period was found to be Rs. 400 per acre which shows that the low fertilizer charges during the economic period. This is evident from the fact that even the medium size farmers used only compost and Suphala from the 8th year onwards. Of the total expenditure of Rs. 4397 per acre spent by the medium size farmers, the expenditure on compost and fertilizers formed only 8.06 percent.

Irrigation Cost

The expenditure on irrigation per acre of coconut garden in case of medium size farmers was Rs. 960 per acre in the 8th year. This is again small as compared to the irrigation cost in any of the year in the establishment period. Thus it is proved that what is applicable to the small size farmers with regard to irrigation cost is also applicable to medium size farmers. The cost of irrigation in the total expenditure was found to be 21.98 percent.

Labour Cost

The expenditure on labour in the 8th year stood at Rs. 900 per acre which is again small as compared to the labour cost in any of year during the establishment period. The expenditure on labour in the 8th year constituted about 20.61 percent of the total expenditure.

COST OF CULTIVATION IN CASE OF LARGE SIZE FARMERS (IRRIGATED)

ESTABLISHMENT PERIOD

Like small and medium size farmers, the large size farmers are also required to spend large amount of money during the first seven years i.e. establishment period. From the Table-4.6, it can be seen that the total expenditure of the large size farmers in the first year amounted to Rs. 5464 per acre. This is found to be very high as compared to the other six years in the establishment period. The reasons as mentioned in the previous section are the investment on the one time expenditure like land preparation, leveling, planting, bunding, cost of seedlings etc. The total amount spent during the establishment period is Rs. 20885 per acre. The cost in the subsequent years of establishment period show a declining trend. However, the expenditure in the seventh year is more as compared to the previous years. This is mainly due to the extra amount spent on the fertilizers in the seventh to keep the crop healthy in the economic phase.

During the first year, a total of Rs. 1386 was spent on labour. This amounts to 25.37 percent of the total expenditure. Irrigation charges in the first year amounted to Rs. 1650 constituting 30.20 percent of the total expenditure during the first year. Again on fertilizers and manures, the large size farmers spent Rs. 249 per acre which worked out to be 4.56 percent of the total expenditure. Thus it is clear that during the first year even the large farmers spent more on irrigation and labour than the fertilizers. The tendency among the coconut farmers in the district is to apply less fertilizer during the first year. This is due to the belief that chemical fertilizers would do more than do good during the first year of the plantation.

Itemwise expenditure during the establishment period shows that major expenditure during the first seven years as in the other two categories are on labour, irrigation and fertilizers and compost. Moisture conservation methods like husk burial are very cheap method to conserve the water content in the soil. The husk is storng in nature and when buried in the soil absorbs and retains moisture which becomes available to roots[3]. The farmers of this area are found to be ignorant about such method of conserving moisture. As a result, the irrigation cost of the coconut plantation in the study area is found to be high.

Material Cost

Fertiliser cost during the first seven years of the coconut plantation shows that the expenditure on the fertilizers and manures vary widely. Thus in case of large farmers the fertilizer and manure cost was found to be Rs. 2679 per acre, accounting for 12.83 percent of the total expenditure of the establishment period.

Irrigation Cost

During the first seven years or establishment period, the large size farmers spent Rs. 10860 per acre only on irrigation. The cost of irrigation during the establishment period thus forms 52.00 percent of the total expenditure. The cost of irrigation could be brought down considerably during

Table 4.6: Per Acre Cost of Cultivation of Coconut in Case of Large Farmers (Irrigated), 1994-95

(Qty in numbers) (Values in Rs.)

ITEMS OF EXPENDITURE	Year of Establishment Period														Total	Economic Period	
	I		II		III		IV		V		VI		VII			VIII	
	Qty	Val	Qty	Val	Qty	Val	Qty	Val	Qty	Val	Qty	Val	Qty	Val		Qty	Val
(A) Material Cost:																	
1. (a) Seedlings @ Rs.30/ seedlings	47	1410	4	120	2	60	-	-	-	-	-	-	-	-	1590	-	-
(b) Supports @ Rs.2.00/ supports	47	94	4	8	2	4	-	-	-	-	-	-	-	-	106	-	-
2. **Compost** (Rs.390/ tractor load)	0.40	152	0.30	114	0.40	152	0.53	201	0.05	247	0.66	250	0.67	255	1372	0.60	228
3. **Fertilizers**																	
Suphala (Rs.5.92/Kg)	9.75	58	12.75	73	11.50	68	19	112	25	148	28	168	29	172	798	10	59
Super Phosphate (Rs.3.02/Kg)	12.80	39	22	66	12.25	37	-	-	-	-	-	-	10.45	32	174	-	-
Muriate of Potash (Rs.3.90/Kg)	-	-	19	74	10.75	42	-	-	-	-	-	-	11.20	44	160	-	-
Urea (Rs. 3.40/Kg)	-	-	15	51	14	48	-	-	-	-	-	-	15	51	150	-	-
Neem Cake (Rs.2.50/Kg)	-	-	-	-	10	25	-	-	-	-	-	-	-	-	-	-	-
4. Read earth (Rs.55/tractor load)	2.25	113	0.25	13	-	-	-	-	-	-	-	-	-	-	126	25	-
5. Sand ((Rs. 50/tractor load)	2.50	150	0.50	25	-	-	-	-	-	-	-	-	-	-	175	-	-
6. Plant protection chemical (B.H.C. Rs. 48/Kg)	0.5	24	1.00	48	1	48	1.10	53	1.20	58	1	48	1.00	48	327	1.00	48

[contd...]

Table 4.6: [contd...]

(Qty in numbers) (Values in Rs.)

ITEMS OF EXPENDITURE	Years of Establishment Period														Total	Economic Period	
	I		II		III		IV		V		VI		VII			VIII	
	Qty	Val	Qty	Val	Qty	Val	Qty	Val	Qty	Val	Qty	Val	Qty	Val		Qty	Val
(B) Irrigation Cost:																	
(a) Cost of irrigation (NO.) Rs. 120/irrigation	11	1320	10	1200	10	1200	11	1320	10	1200	10	1200	11	1320	8760	8	960
(C) Labour Cost:																	
1. Land Preparation	1.25	188	-	-	-	-	-	-	-	-	-	-	-	-	188	-	-
(a) Tractor Service (Rs.50/hours)																	
(b) Levelling (Rs. 40/bullock pair per day)	5	200	-	-	-	-	-	-	-	-	-	-	-	-	200	-	-
(c) Bunding (Rs. 30/mandayas)	9	270	-	-	-	-	-	-	-	-	-	-	-	-	270	-	-
2. Digging Pits (contact at Rs. 8/pit)	47	376	-	-	-	-	-	-	-	-	-	-	-	-	376	-	-
3. Planting (Rs.30/mandays)	6	180	-	-	-	-	-	-	-	-	-	-	-	-	180	-	-
4. Application of compost & fertilizers (Rs. 30/mandays)	3	90	2	60	3	90	2	60	3	90	2	60	1	30	480	2	60
5. Plant protection (Rs. 30/mandays)	2	60	1	30	2	60	1	30	2	60	2	60	2	60	360	1	30

[contd...]

Table 4.6: [contd...]

(Qty in numbers) (Values in Rs.)

ITEMS OF EXPENDITURE	Year of Establishment Period														Total	Economic Period	
	I		II		III		IV		V		VI		VII			VIII	
	Qty	Val	Qty	Val	Qty	Val	Qty	Val	Qty	Val	Qty	Val	Qty	Val		Qty	Val
6. Weeding & widening of basins (Rs. 30/mandays)	7	210	3	90	3	90	3	90	3	90	4	120	3	90	780	3	90
7. Permanent Labour for both	-	330	8	240	10	300	11	330	10	300	10	300	10	300	2100	8	240
8. Irrigating (Rs. 30/mandays) watch & ward and harvesting	11	200	-	245	-	250	-	260	-	280	-	300	-	375	1910	-	450
Total of A + B +C	-	5464	-	2457	-	2474	-	2457	-	2473	-	2504	-	2777	20607	-	2165
Interest on amount invested during the previous year (10%)	-	-	-	546	-	246	-	247	-	246	-	247	-	250	278	-	2089
Total cost during the year		5464		3003		2720		2704		2719		2751		3027	20885		4254

Source: Field Survey.

N.B. : Figures in value column are rounded off

the nut bearing stage by adopting moisture conservation methods mentioned above. If irrigation cost (which constitutes about 52 percent) is brought down, the total expenditure would be reduced considerably benefiting the farmers.

Labour Cost

It may be seen from the table that the labour cost in the establishment period was Rs. 4356 per acre. This excludes the number of mandays of labour used for irrigation as the number of mandays involved for irrigation has been added to the cost of irrigation. In case of the large size farmers in the study area, the per acre labour cost involved in bringing up the coconut garden was found to be more than 20.86 percent of the total expenditure during the first seven years.

ECONOMIC PERIOD

Material Cost

The large size farmers spent Rs. 287 per acre on compost and fertilizers. The expenditure on fertilizer is least in case of the large size farmers as compared to other size groups mainly due to the economy of scale in purchasing materials in large quantity. The large size farmers also applied compost and Suphala only in the 8th year. The percentage of expenditure on compost and fertilizers in case of large size farmers in the total cost of cultivation in the 8th year was found to be 6.75 percent.

Irrigation Cost

In case of large size farmers per acre cost of irrigation in the 8th year stood at Rs. 960 which formed 22. 57 percent of the total expenditure. Irrigation cost as in the case for other two categories, has declined even in case of large size farmers in the 8th year.

Labour Cost

Labour cost in case of large size farmers in the 8th year stood at Rs. 870 per acre accounting for 20.45 percent of the total expenditure. Thus labour cost also has declined considerably during the 8th year which is the first year of the economic period.

COST OF CULTIVATION IN CASE OF SMALL FARMERS (UNIRRIGATED)

An attempt has also been made to know the performance of irrigated farmers in the study region. The study revealed many interesting aspects about coconut cultivation in the unirrigated plantations. A detailed survey was conducted and with the information collected from such farmers, a cost analysis has been carried out. The item wise cost information is presented in the Table 4.7. The expenditure of unirrigated farms is found to be low as compared to the irrigated ones. There are many reasons for this. The farmers in the unirrigated sector did not apply sufficient quantity of chemical fertilizers to bring up their gardens, used less green manures, reduced the cost of watering the coconut trees. Water forms a very important production factor in coconut cultivation and the coconut plantation cannot survive without water for long time. Further if there is a low productivity it can be directly attributed to non-availability of water. Here the term unirrigated may be taken in the sense that the farmers did not make any special provisions like tube wells or canals etc to irrigate the plantation. Watering of the plants was done mainly through pot watering.

Cost of cultivation in case of unirrigated plantation is also analysed much in the same way as it is done in case of the irrigated plantations. The life span of the coconut is divided in to two periods i.e. the establishment period and the economic period.

ESTABLISHMENT PERIOD

The total cost of cultivation in case of unirrigated small farmers during the first year of the establishment period was found to be Rs. 4421 per acre. This works out to be lower as compared to that of the small farmers of the irrigated region. The reasons of this are due to the non-application of chemical fertilizers application of green manure in smaller quantity, and lower cost of watering the plants. The total expenditure for the seven years of establishment period was found to be Rs. 16638 per acre and the expenditure during the first year stood at 26.57 percent. The expenditure from the second year to the seventh year ranged from 13.45 percent to 14.49 percent.

Table 4.7: Per Acre Cost of Cultivation of Coconut in Case of Small Farmers (Irrigated), 1994-95

(Qty in numbers) (Values in Rs.)

ITEMS OF EXPENDITURE	Year of Establishment Period														Total	Economic Period	
	I		II		III		IV		V		VI		VII			VIII	
	Qty	Val	Qty	Val	Qty	Val	Qty	Val	Qty	Val	Qty	Val	Qty	Val		Qty	Val
(A) **Material Cost:**		–															
1. (a) **Seedlings** @ Rs.31/ seedlings	47	1457	3	93	2	62	1	31	-	-	-	-	-	-	1643	-	-
(b) Supports @ Rs.2.00/ supports	47	94	3	6	2	4	1	31	-	-	-	-	-	-	105	-	-
2. Compost (Rs.400/ tractor load)	0.30	120	0.32	128	0.38	152	0.42	168	0.48	192	0.48	192	0.50	200	1152	0.47	188
3. Red earth (Rs.55/tractor load)	2.00	110	1	55	-	-	-	-	-	-	-	-	-	-	165	-	-
4. Sand (Rs.55/tractor load)	2.00	110	-	-	-	-	-	-	-	-	-	-	-	-	110	-	-
5. Plant protection chemical (B.H.C. Rs. 48/Kg)	0.5	24	0.5	24	0.70	34	0.80	40	0.85	41	0.86	41	0.90	43	247	0.5	24
B. Irrigation Cost:																	
1. Irrigation (pot irrigation mandays)	31	930	33	990	38	1140	40	1200	41	1230	42	1260	43	1290	8040	30	900
(C) **Labour Cost:**																	
(a) Land Preparation (Rs.40/bullock pair per day)	5	200	-	-	-	-	-	-	-	-	-	-	-	-	200	-	-
(b) Levelling (Rs. 40/bullock pair per day)	4	160	-	-	-	-	-	-	-	-	-	-	-	-	160	-	-
(c) Bunding (Rs. 30/mandayas)	8	240	-	-	-	-	-	-	-	-	-	-	-	-	240	-	-

[contd...]

Table 4.7: [contd...]

(Qty in numbers) (Values in Rs.)

ITEMS OF EXPENDITURE	Year of Establishment Period														Total	Economic Period	
	I		II		III		IV		V		VI		VII			VIII	
	Qty	Val	Qty	Val	Qty	Val	Qty	Val	Qty	Val	Qty	Val	Qty	Val		Qty	Val
2. Digging Pits (contact at Rs. 8/pit)	47	376	-	-	-	-	-	-	-	-	-	-	-	-	376	-	-
3. Planting (Rs.30/mandays)	6	180	-	-	-	-	-	-	-	-	-	-	-	-	180	-	-
4. Application of compost & fertilizers (Rs. 30/mandays)	3	90	4	120	4	120	3	90	3	90	3	90	4	120	920	2	60
5. Plant protection	2	60	2	60	3	90	2	60	2	60	2	60	3	90	480	1	30
6. Weeding & widening of basins (Rs. 30/mandays)	3	90	4	120	4	120	3	90	3	90	3	90	3	90	690	3	90
7. Permanent Labour for both watch & ward and harvesting (Rs. 30/mandays)	-	180	-	200	-	230	-	280	-	300	-	350	-	370	1910	-	400
Total of A + B +C	-	4421	-	1796	-	1952	-	1990	-	2003	-	2083	-	2203	16418	-	1692
Interest on amount invested during the previous year (10%)	-	-	-	442	-	180	-	195	-	199	-	200	-	208	220	-	1664
Total cost during the year		4421		2238		2132		2185		2202		2283		2411	16638		3356

Source: Field Survey.

N.B. : Figures in value column are rounded off

Material Cost

Reasonably a good proportion of the expenditure was made on compost during the first seven years. The total expenditure incurred on the application of compost was Rs. 1152 per acre and this constituted a mere 6.92 percent of the total expenditure. The application of compost during the seven years showed an increasing trend. Further an expenditure of Rs. 1643 towards seedlings has been added to the total cost of cultivation.

Irrigation Cost (Pot irrigation)

As said earlier, pot irrigation has been carried out in the unirrigated areas. The total expense for the seven year period was Rs. 8040 per acre. The expense on irrigation for the seven year period may look very small. However, it should be noted that pot irrigation is usually carried out mainly during the summer months and there is no expense on pot irrigation during the summer months and there is no expense on pot irrigation during the rainy and winter months. The cost of pot irrigation is estimated to be Rs. 8040 per acre constituting 48.32 percent of the total expenditure incurred during the seven year period. It may also be noted that there was no continuous increase or decrease in the expenditure during the seven year period.

Labour Cost

The expenditure on labour during the seven year establishment period was found to be Rs. 4596 per acre. This constitutes 27.62 percent of the total expenditure incurred during the establishment period. Thus labour charges turned out to be a major items of expenditure even in case of unirrigated regions.

ECONOMIC PERIOD

Material cost

The cost of cultivation in case of small farmers in unirrigated plantation also shows a declining trend in the economic phase. The Table reveals that the per acre cost of cultivation per acre during the 8th year was found to be only Rs. 3356 per acre of which the share of manures and fertilizers was a meager amount of Rs. 188. The expenditure on manures in case of unirrigated farmers constituted about 5.60 percent of the total expenditure during the year.

Irrigation Cost (Pot irrigation)

The pot irrigation charges during the first year of the economic period as can be seen from the Table is just Rs. 900 per acre. The expenditure on pot irrigation constituted a lion's share (26.82 percent) in the total expenditure incurred by the small unirrigated farmers during the first year of the economic period.

Labour Cost

The total labour cost in case of unirrigated small farmers stood at Rs. 580 per acre. This constituted 17.28 percent of the total expenditure. The labour cost in the economic period is also found to be lower as compared to any other year in the establishment period.

COST OF CULTIVATION IN CASE OF MEDIUM FARMERS (UNIRRIGATED)

ESTABLISHMENT PERIOD

Material Cost

The expenditure incurred by the medium farmers has also shown much the same pattern as that of the small farmers (Table 4.8). The application of chemical fertilizers here again is nil and main expenditure is on compost. The total expenditure on compost was Rs. 1021 wich constituted 6.64 percent of the total cost of Rs. 15375 incurred during the establishment period. The total expenditure on seedlings was Rs. 1783 per acre amounting to 11.60 percent of the total expenditure during the establishment period.

Irrigation Cost (Pot irrigation)

The cost of pot irrigation in case of the medium size farmers was found to be Rs. 7410 per acre for the seven year period. This again looks minimum as compared to the irrigation charges of the medium size irrigated farmers. Moreover, pot irrigation is usually carried out during the dry months of the year. Even then, the cost of irrigation was found to be 48.20 percent of the total expenditure during the establishment period. Further, a look at the table shows that irrigation cost has recorded a constant increase during the seven year period.

Table 4.8: Per Acre Cost of Cultivation of Coconut in Case of Medium (Unirrigated), Farmers, 1994-95

(Qty in numbers) (Values in Rs.)

ITEMS OF EXPENDITURE	Year of Establishment Period														Total	Economic Period	
	I		II		III		IV		V		VI		VII			VIII	
	Qty	Val	Qty	Val	Qty	Val	Qty	Val	Qty	Val	Qty	Val	Qty	Val		Qty	Val
(A) Material Cost:																	
1. **(a) Seedlings**																	
@ Rs.30.75/ seedlings	47	1445	4	123	3	92	3	92	1	31	-	-	-	-	1784	-	-
(b) Supports																	
@ Rs.2.00/ supports	47	94	4	8	3	6	3	6	1	2	-	-	-	-	116	-	-
2. Compost (Rs.390/ tractor load)	0.28	109	0.30	117	0.32	125	0.38	148	0.40	156	0.46	179	0.48	187	1021	0.40	156
3. Red earth (Rs.55/tractor load)	1.80	95	0.50	26	-	-	-	-	-	-	-	-	-	-	122	-	-
4. Sand (Rs.53/tractor load)	1.79	95	-	-	-	-	-	-	-	-	-	-	-	-	95	-	-
5. Plant protection chemical (B.H.C. Rs. 48/Kg)	0.5	24	0.5	24	0.52	25	0.52	25	0.50	26	0.56	27	0.56	27	178	0.54	26
B. Irrigation Cost:																	
1. Irrigation (pot irrigation mandays)	31	930	32	960	34	1020	35	1050	37	1110	38	1140	40	1200	7410	29	870
(C) Labour Cost:																	
1. (a) Land Preparation (Rs.50/tractor service)	1.25	188	-	-	-	-	-	-	-	-	-	-	-	-	200	-	-
(b) Levelling (Rs. 40/bullock pair per day)	4	160	-	-	-	-	-	-	-	-	-	-	-	-	160	-	-
(c) Bunding (Rs. 30/mandayas)	7	210	-	-	-	-	-	-	-	-	-	-	-	-	210	-	-

[contd...]

Table 4.8: [contd...]

(Qty in numbers) (Values in Rs.)

ITEMS OF EXPENDITURE	Year of Establishment Period														Total	Economic Period	
	I		II		III		IV		V		VI		VII			VIII	
	Qty	Val	Qty	Val	Qty	Val	Qty	Val	Qty	Val	Qty	Val	Qty	Val		Qty	Val
2. Digging Pits (contact at Rs. 8/pit)	47	376	-	-	-	-	-	-	-	-	-	-	-	-	376	-	-
3. Planting (Rs.30/mandays)	6	180	-	-	-	-	-	-	-	-	-	-	-	-	180	-	-
4. Application of compost & fertilizers (Rs. 30/mandays)	2	60	3	90	3	90	2	60	3	90	3	90	3	90	570	2	60
5. Plant protection	2	60	1	30	2	60	2	60	1	30	2	60	2	60	360	2	60
6. Weeding & widening of basins (Rs. 30/mandays)	3	90	2	60	2	60	3	90	3	60	3	90	3	90	540	3	90
7. Permanent Labour for both watch & ward and harvesting (Rs. 30/mandays)	-	180	-	190	-	210	-	260	-	300	-	340	-	370	1850	-	400
Total of A + B +C	-	4296	-	1629	-	1688	-	1791	-	1805	-	1926	-	2024	15171	-	1662
Interest on amount invested during the previous year (10%)	-	-	-	430	-	163	-	169	-	179	-	181	-	193	202	-	1537
Total cost during the year		4296		2059		1851		1960		1984		2107		2217	15375		3199

Source : Field Survey.

N.B.: Figures in value column are rounded ofl.

Labour Cost

The expense on labour for the seven year period stood at Rs. 4086 per acre. Thus the expenditure on labour during the establishment period worked out to be 26.58 percent of the total expenditure. Here again the expenditure on labour was high during the first year and the reasons as explained earlier are due to the charges on bunding, ground leveling etc.

ECONOMIC PERIOD

Material Cost

On an average, a medium size unirrigated farmers spent Rs. 156 per acre on manures. To be specific the unirrigated farmers in the sample area applied only compost for bringing up their garden. The cost on compost was found to be 4.88 percent of the total expenditure incurred during the first year of economic period.

Irrigation Cost (Pot irrigation)

The cost of pot irrigation during the first year of the economic period in case of the medium farmers was Rs. 870 per acre amounting to 27.29 percent of the total expenditure during the 8th year.

Labour Cost

The expenditure on labour in case of the medium size unirrigated farmers during the 8th year was Rs. 610 per acre which works out to 19.07 percent of the total expenditure incurred during that year. From the above, it is clear that even in case of the medium farmers, the cost of cultivation began to decline in the economic period.

COST OF CULTIVATION IN CASE OF LARGE FARMERS (UNIRRIGATED)

ESTABLISHMENT PERIOD

Material Cost

The large size farmers had relatively a lower expenditure on compost than their counter parts- medium and small size farmers in the unirrigated category. The total expenditure per acre for compost during the establishment period was only Rs. 962 constituting only 6.49 percent of the total expenditure. Further, the expense on seedlings in case of large farmers stood at Rs. 1800 per acre amounting to 12.14 percent of total expenditure.

Irrigation Cost (Pot irrigation)

The pot irrigation charges in case of the large farmers was also less as compared to their counter parts in the medium and small size unirrigated sector. A total expenditure of Rs. 7110 was incurred for this purpose showing 47.96 percent of the total expenditure. Thus on pot irrigation a large amount of money has been spent by the large size unirrigated farmers.

Labour Cost

Labour cost in the establishment period in case of the large size farmer stood at Rs. 3936 per acre which is 26.55 percent of the total expenditure. The expenditure on labour showed a similar trend as in the case of the other two categories.

ECONOMIC PERIOD

Material Cost

The large size unirrigated farmers spent Rs. 144 per acre on compost during the 8th year. This constituted 4.68 percent of the total expenditure. Here again the large size farmers have the advantage of the economy of scale as compared to the other two categories. The large farmers like the other two categories in the unirrigated sector, spent only on compost.

Irrigation Cost (Pot irrigation)

The expenditure incurred by the large size unirrigated farmers on pot irrigation during the 8th year was Rs. 810 per acre. This constituted 26.37 percent of the total expenditure.

Labour Cost

The expenditure incurred by the large size unirrigated farmers on labour during the 8th year was Rs. 610. This constituted 19.86 percent of the total expenditure.

Table 4.9: Per Acre Cost of Cultivation of Coconut in Case of Large Farmers (Unirrigated), 1994-95

(Qty in numbers) (Values in Rs.)

ITEMS OF EXPENDITURE	Years of Establishment Period														Total	Economic Period	
	I		II		III		IV		V		VI		VII			VIII	
	Qty	Val	Qty	Val	Qty	Val	Qty	Val	Qty	Val	Qty	Val	Qty	Val		Qty	Val
(A) Material Cost:																	
1. **(a) Seedlings** @ Rs.30/seedlings	47	1410	3	90	4	120	4	120	2	60	-	-	-	-	1800	-	-
(b) Supports @ Rs.2.00/ supports	47	94	3	6	4	8	4	8	2	4	-	-	-	-	120	-	-
2. Compost (Rs.380/tractor load)	0.29	110	0.30	114	0.32	122	0.35	133	0.37	141	0.40	152	0.50	190	962	0.38	144
3. Red earth (Rs.50/tractor load)	1.50	75	0.50	25	-	-	-	-	-	-	-	-	-	-	100	-	-
4. Sand (Rs.50/tractor load)	1.60	80	-	-	-	-	-	-	-	-	-	-	-	-	80	-	-
5. Plant protection chemical (B.H.C. Rs. 45/Kg)	0.5	24	0.5	24	0.52	25	0.52	25	0.54	26	0.56	26	0.58	28	178	0.54	25
B. Irrigation Cost:																	
1. Irrigation (pot irrigation mandays)	30	900	31	930	32	960	34	1020	35	1050	37	1110	38	1140	7110	26	810
(C) Labour Cost:																	
1. Land Preparation (a) (Tractor Service Rs.150/tractor load)	1.25	188	-	-	-	-	-	-	-	-	-	-	-	-	188	-	-
(b) Levelling (Rs. 40/bullock pair per day)	4	160	-	-	-	-	-	-	-	-	-	-	-	-	160	-	-
(c) Bunding (Rs. 30/mandayas)	7	210	-	-	-	-	-	-	-	-	-	-	-	-	210	-	-

[contd...]

Table 4.8: [contd...]

(Qty in numbers) (Values in Rs.)

ITEMS OF EXPENDITURE	Year of Establishment Period														Total	Economic Period	
	I		II		III		IV		V		VI		VII			VIII	
	Qty	Val	Qty	Val	Qty	Val	Qty	Val	Qty	Val	Qty	Val	Qty	Val		Qty	Val
2. Digging Pits (contact at Rs. 8/pit)	47	376	-	-	-	-	-	-	-	-	-	-	-	-	376	-	-
3. Planting (Rs.30/mandays)	6	180	-	-	-	-	-	-	-	-	-	-	-	-	180	-	-
4. Application of compost & fertilizers (Rs. 30/mandays)	2	60	2	60	3	90	2	60	2	60	2	60	2	60	450	2	60
5. Plant protection (Rs. 30/mandays)	2	60	1	30	2	60	1	30	1	30	2	60	1	30	300	2	60
6. Weeding & widening of basins (Rs. 30/mandays)	3	90	2	60	2	60	3	90	3	90	3	90	3	90	570	3	90
7. Permanent Labour for both watch & ward and harvesting (Rs. 30/mandays)	-	180	-	200	-	210	-	260	-	300	-	340	-	360	1850	-	400
Total of A + B +C	-	4197	-	1539	-	1655	-	1746	-	1761	-	1838	-	1898	14634	-	1590
Interest on amount invested during the previous year (10%)	-	-	-	420	-	154	-	165	-	175	-	176	-	184	190	-	1482
Total cost during the year		4197		1959		1809		1912		1936		2014		2082	14824		3072

Source : Field Survey.

N.B.: Figures in value column are rounded off.

Thus from the analysis of both irrigated and unirrigated farmers, it is quite clear that economic period is characterized by low cost of cultivation and bulk of the investment has to be made during the establishment period. The analysis also makes it clear that the cost of cultivation in the study area is found to be low as compared to the cost in other part of the country.

REFERENCES

1. Shastri, K.N.R.M.G., Chandrakanth R. Nagaraj: Economic considerations in selecting coconut enterprise, *Journal of Plantation Crops*, Vol.15, No.1, 1987, pp 15 - 22.
2. Thampan, P.K. : *Profitable Coconut Growing*, Coconut Development Board, Ministry of Agriculture, Govt. of India, Cochin-11, Kerala, India, 1986, pp 1 - 58.
3. Jose Abraham, T.S.S. Rawther, P.M. Jacob and Robert Cecil: Trend in Yield of Root Affected Coconut Palm, *Journal of Plantation Crops*, Vol.15, No.6, 1984, pp 38 - 43.

CHAPTER 5

PRODUCTION OF COCONUT

In the present Chapter, the production of coconut in the sample area has been analysed. The production estimates are done in case of small, medium and large size farmers in the irrigated and unirrigated coconut plantations. The study points out many interesting and encouraging results regarding the production of coconut in sample area.

PRODUCTION OF COCONUT

Coconut is consumed in three different form. They are - Tender coconut, Desiccated coconut and copra.

Tender Coconut

The tender coconut is considered to be a popular refreshing drink and supplies a satisfactory beverage. The tender nut water is laxative and has diuretic properties[1]. At the tender stage, the nut is used mainly for drinking purposes. The coconut water at this stage contains a maximum concentration of carbohydrates of about 5 percent, which drops on maturity to around 2 percent[2]. Coconut water has been used for centuries in the countries of origin as remedy for various ailments. Occasionally by itself or often mixed with coconut milk, it has been used to treat intestinal worms and relieve stomach troubles and it is said to be particularly useful in cholera cases, at the presence of sailnes and albumins checks vomiting. It is also said to diminish rashes caused by small-pox, chicken-pox and measles and is thought to be generally beneficial to the skin[3].

Desiccated Coconut

Desiccated coconut is the dried disintegrated white

kernel of the coconut, processed under strict hygienic conditions for human consumption. It remains, for the most part, the original oil and protein of the fresh nut. It is produced in four standard grades-extra fine, fine, medium and coarse - as well as in many fancy cuts, including threads, strips, chips, slices and shreds[4]. The meat of the mature coconut is used in a number of ways. It may be eaten as it is, but more often it is grated for direct use in the preparation of various food dishes. Alternatively it is pressed, with or without water, to extract coconut milk[5].

In factories producing desiccated coconut the combined coconut water and milk is collected in tanks, and the so called "drain oil" is extracted from the oily scum and used in soap making, the residual press cake being used as fertilizer[6].

Desiccated coconut used in confectionary, biscuits and cooking and is prepared only from the best-grade nuts. The moisture content is lower than that of copra, and the oil content is slightly higher[7].

Copra

The dried kernel is a major source of vegetable oil, when milled. Copra yields coconut oil which is used extensively as both an edible and a technical oil and copra cake, a valuable animal feed, is particularly useful in the feeding of dairy cattle. The hard shell is mainly consumed locally as a fuel, but some quantity is carbonized into charcoal[8].

PRODUCTION OF COCONUT IN THE SAMPLE AREA

The Table-5.1 provides the details of total production and productivity of tender, desiccated coconut and copra by the sample farmers in both the irrigated and unirrigated plantation.

Out of the total irrigated area of 426.38 acres under coconut cultivation in the sample area, 48.03 acres are held by small farmers, 130.35 acres and 248 acres are held by medium and large farmers respectively. Thus the area held by the small farmers was 11.26 percent of the total area under coconut cultivation. The medium and large farmers held 30.57 percent and 58.16 percent respectively.

The total production by all types of farmers in the irrigated plantation during the year 1994-95 stood at 1165103 nuts. Out of the total production, the contribution of small farmers was 144042 nuts. Thus the contribution of the small farmers in the total production stood at 12.36 percent. The contribution of the small farmers in the total production is good considering the fact that their share in the total cultivated area. The total produce from the medium farmers was 362373 nuts amounting to 31.10 percent of the total production. Here again the share of land under the medium farmers is less as compared to the area under large farmers. The production by the medium farmers is also good since it has only 30.57 percent of the total area and contributes 31.10 percent.

The large farmers have produced 658688 nuts accounting for 56.53 precent. Comparing the area held by the large farmers, their production is low. This is mainly due to better farm management by small and medium size farmers as compared to that of the large farmers.

Table 5.1 : Area Production and Productivity of the Sample Farmers, 1994-95

Sl. No.	Type of Farmer	Irrigated			Unirrigated		
		Area (in acres)	Produ-ction in nuts)	Produc-tivity in nuts)	Area acres)	Produ-ction in nuts)	Produc-tivity in nuts)
1.	Small	48.03	144042	2999	29.78	63134	2120
		(11.26)	(12.36)		(19.48)	(20.50)	
2.	Medium	130.35	362373	2780	47.10	95613	2030
		(30.57)	(31.10)		(30.81)	(31.04)	
3.	Large	248.00	658688	2656	76.00	149264	1964
		(58.16)	(56.53)		(49.71)	(48.46)	
	Total	426.38	1165103	2733	152.88	308011	2015
		(100.00)	(100.00)		(100.00)	(100.00)	

Source: Field Survey.

N.B. : Figures in brakets represent the percentages to the total

The Table-5.1 also shows the productivity per acre in case of small, medium and large farmers. Productivity per acre is calculated by dividing the total produce by the area. It is clear from the table that small farmers have better productivity as compared to that of medium and large farms. The productivity was observed to be 2999 nuts per acre in case of small farms. The productivity in case of medium and large farmers was found to be 2780 nutsand 2656 nuts per acre respectively. Thus small farmers have better productivity as compared to medium and large farmers in the sample area.

The total area under unirrigated coconut plantation category as shown in the table is 152.88 acres. The share of small size farmers in the total unirrigated area under coconut plantation is 19.48 percent and the shares of medium and large farmers are 30.81 percent and 49.71 percent respectively. The total production in the unirrigated lands during the year 1994-95 was 308011 nuts. Of the total production, 63134 was produced by the small farms. The production by the medium and large farms amounted to 95613 nuts and 149264 nuts respectively. In case of the small and medium farms the production is almost in proportion to the area under the forms. The area under the small forms was 19.48 percent and contributed 20.50 percent of the total produce. In the same way, the area under medium farmers was 30.81 percent and contributed 31.04 percent of the total produce. The area under large farms in unirrigated category was 49.71 productivity of the unirrigated farms was low as compared to the irrigated farms. The productivity in case of the small farms stood at 2120 nuts per acre and that of medium and large farms stood at 2030 nuts and 1964 nuts per acre respectively. Thus as in the case of irrigated coconut farms, the table shows that the productivity of unirrigated small farmers was found to be higher as compared to that of the large and medium farmers. Here also due to better management, the small farms could produce more per unit area.

The productivity of coconut plantations as analysed above points out to the fact that productivity in Tumkur is much higher than the national average and also the productivity levels of some of the major coconut producing states like Andhra Pradesh, Kerala and Tamil Nadu. Further the average productivity in the sample area (6752 nuts per hectare) is found to be higher than that of the State average. The average productivity in India during 1950-51 was 5759 nuts per hectare, which increased to

6532 nuts during 1951-56 and thereafter productivity was found to be declining steadily throughout. Thus national average productivity worked out to be 5894 nuts per hectare in the sample area in case of irrigated plantation. However, in case of unirrigated coconut farms the average productivity of 4978 nuts hectare was lower than the national average. In Kerala[9] the average productivity of 6917 per hectare during 1955-56 decreased to 5617 nuts during 1965-66 and to 4964 nuts and 4792 nuts during 1975-76 and 1985-86 respectively. It is clear that the productivity in case of irrigated farms in the sample area was observed to be higher than that of any other area in the country and hence coconut farming in Tumkur district provides better yield to the farmers.

Production of Tender, Desiccated Coconut and Copra

The Table-5.2 gives a detail picture of the item wise production of coconut namely tender, desiccated coconut and copra by different size groups farmers in the irrigated and unirrigated farms.

Out of the total production of 1165103 coconuts produced in the irrigated farms 119205 coconuts were taken as Tender Coconuts, 225268 nuts were used as desiccated coconuts and 820630 nuts are copra during the year 1994-95. The quantity of coconut produced as Tender coconut in the sample area formed 10.23 percent of the total production. Desiccated coconut and coconut used for the production of copra formed 19.33 percent and 70.43 percent of the total production respectively. Thus the major proportion of coconuts produced in the Tumkur district was used in the production of copra which is used for oil extraction.

The share of small farmers in the total production of tender coconut was 38.93 percent. This point is worth noting as the small farmers having 11.36 percent of the total land area under coconut farming accounted for 38.93 percent of the Tender coconut. Further the table reveals that out of a total of 144042 coconut produced by small farms, the share of small farmers in the total production of tender coconut was 38.93 percent. This point is worth noting as the small farmers having 11.36 percent of the total land area under coconut farming accounted for 38.93 percent of the Tender coconut. Further the table reveals that out of a total of 144042 coconut produced by small farms during 1994-95, 46410 nuts were harvested as Tender coconut. Thus a total of 32.22 percent of the total produce by the small farms was harvested in the tender stage. It may be noted here that the price of tender coconut is lower than the price of desiccated coconut and copra. The desiccated coconut and copra production by the small farms were found to be 40 percent and 27.78 percent respectively. Further, if total production is considered the share of the small farmers in the production of desiccated coconut was only 25.58 percent and that of copra was 4.88 percent. Thus the table reveals that the small farmer in the sample area are interested more in selling tender coconut than the other two items. The reason for this as evolved from the field survey is that the small farmers are found to be in urgent need of money and cannot wait till the maturity of coconut. However a few farmers in this area were of the opinion that productivity of coconut increase with the harvest of tender coconut.

The medium farmers had a total production of 362373 nuts in the year 1994-95 of which 43484 nuts were harvested early in the form of tender coconut. Thus medium farmers having 31.10 percent of the total land area under coconut plantations contributed 36.48 percent of the total production of tender coconut. The figures in Table-5.2 show that the medium farmer's production of desiccated coconut (65227) is slightly higher than that of tender coconut (43484) and the share of coconut used for producing copra is found to be increased reasonably. This can be considered as a good trend as desiccated coconut and copra fetch better prices to the farmers. However, the figures show that the harvesting of tender coconut has still remained higher at 12 percent. Out of the total production of 362373 coconut by the medium farmers, 43484 nuts were harvested as tender coconuts. Thus tender coconuts formed 12 percent of the total production of coconuts by medium farmers. The share of desiccated coconut and copra formed 18 percent and 70 percent of the total produce. An average of 600 nuts are required for the production of one quintal of copra in this region. The medium farmers

Table 5.2: Production of Tender, Desiccated Coconut and Copra by Different Size Group of Farmers, 1994-95

(Nuts in numbers)

Sl. No.	Type of Farmer	Irrigated				Unirrigated			
		Tender Coconut	Desiccated Coconut	Copra	Total Percentage	Tender Coconut	Desiccated Coconut	Copra	Total Percentage
1.	Small	46410	57616	40016	144042	22841	27488	12805	63134
		[32.23]	[40.0]	[27.78]	[100]	[36.18]	[43.54]	[20.28]	[100]
		(38.93)	(25.58)	(04.88)	(12.36)	(41.90)	(39.33)	(06.97)	(20.50)
2.	Medium	43484	65227	253662	362373	18950	19294	57368	95612
		[12.00]	[18.0]	[70.0]	[10.00]	[11.82]	[20.18]	[60.00]	[100]
		(36.48)	(28.96)	(30.91)	(31.10)	(34.77)	(27.61)	(31.24)	(31.04)
3.	Large	29311	102425	526952	658688	12717	23106	113442	149265
		[04.45]	[15.55]	[80.0]	[100]	[08.52]	[15.48]	[76.00]	[100]
		(24.59)	(45.47)	(64.21)	(56.53)	(23.33)	(33.06)	(61.78)	(48.46)
	Total	119205	225268	820630	1165103	54508	69888	183615	308011
		[10.23]	[19.33]	[70.43]	[100]	[17.70]	[22.69]	[59.61]	[100]
		(100)	(100)	(100)	(100)	(100)	(100)	(100)	(100)

Source: Field Survey.

N.B. : Figures in round brackets represent the column percentage to the total,
Figures in square brackets represent the row percentages to the total

having less requirement for money in the short run, are in a better position to wait for the coconut to mature and sell in it in the form of desiccated coconut and copra. As a result of this, the earnings of the medium farmers are found to be higher as compared to that of the small farmers.

The large farmers with irrigation had a total production of 658688 coconut during the year 1994-95, and out of which 29311 nuts were harvested in the form of tender coconut. As can be seen from the Table-5.2 the production of tender coconut in terms of number and percentage was lower in case of the large farmers as compared to the other two categories. However, it should be noted here that the large farmers had a share of 58.16 percent of the total land area under coconut cultivation (Table-5.1). Out of the total production of 658688 nuts by the large farmers, 29311 nuts were harvested as tender coconut. This constituted about 4.45 percent of the total produce by the large farmers. Further the number of desiccated coconut stood at 102425 and that of coconut used for the production of copra stood at 526952 constituting 15.5 percent and 80 percent respectively. Thus production of copra by the large farmers stood at the highest level as compared to other two categories. From the table it can be seen that the total production of nuts used for copra by the large farmers in the sample area was 526952 nuts. This constituted 64.21 percent of the total production of copra by all the three categories farmers during the year 1994-95. The high proportion of production of copra by the large farmers is a good sign as the sale of coconut in the form of copra would bring them higher income as compared to the other two items.

In the unirrigated plantation, the small farmers produced 22841 tender coconut in the year 1994-95. Small farmers in unirrigated plantation have a total share of 19.48 percent of the total area under coconut in to unirrigated cultivation (Table-5.1). The share of the small farmers in the total production of tender coconut in the unirrigated cultivation was found to be 41.90 percent which is higher even when we compare it to the small irrigated farmer. The production of desiccated coconut by the unirrigated farmers was 39.33 percent of the total produce by the three categories. Further the production of copra stood at 12805 nuts by the small farmers accounting 6.97 percent of the total production of copra by the three categories of farmers. Thus it is clear that the share of production of desiccated coconut and copra by the small farmer in the unirrigated sector was meagre. Of the total production 63134 coconuts by the small unirrigated farmers, 22841 nuts were harvested as tender coconut. This formed 36.18 percent of the total produce. The total number of desiccated coconut produced by the small farmers was 27488 constituting 43.54 percent of the total produce. Copra production by the small farmers in the unirrigated sector was meagre accounting for only 20.28 percent of the total produce.

The medium farmers in the unirrigated farms produced 95613 coconuts in the year 1994-95, of which 18950 nuts were harvested as tender coconuts. The total production of tender coconut by the medium farmers formed 34.77 percent of the total production of tender coconut by the three categories of farmers in the unirrigated sector. The production of desiccated coconut by medium farmers stood at 19294 constituting 27.61 percent of the total desiccated production. The production of copra by the medium farmers again stood at 31.24 percent of the total copra production in the unirrigated sector. Out of the total 95614 coconuts produced by the medium farmers, tender nuts were 18950 forming 19.82 percent. The desiccated coconut and copra in the total production stood at 19294 nuts and 57368 nuts constituting 20.18 percent and 60 percent respectively. Thus the medium farmers in unirrigated sector also showed a similar tendency like their counter part in the irrigated sector. The reduction in the scale of tender coconut and increase in the sale of other two items would help the farmers to a great extent to earn more income.

The large farmers in the unirrigated sector possessing 49.21 percent (Table-5.1) of the total land, produced 149264 nuts in the year 1994-95. The harvest of tender coconut stood at 23.33 percent of the total tender coconut produced by all the three types of farmers. Similarly the production of desiccated coconut was 23106 which formed 33.06 percent of the total desiccated coconut produced by the three categories. Further 113442 nuts of copra were produced by the large unirrigated farmers. This formed 61.78 percent of the total copra produce by all the three categories.

Of the total production of 149264 nuts produced by the large size unirrigated farmers, 12717 nuts were harvested as tender coconut. Thus the share of tender coconut in their total production stood at only 8.52 percent. The production of desiccated coconut and copra was 23106 nuts and 13442 nuts accounting for 15.48 percent and 76 percent respectively.

From the analysis of unirrigated farmers, it may be noticed that the production of copra and desiccated coconut was low as compared to that of the irrigated farmers. The reason for this as given by the farmers, is that quality of copra and desiccated coconut produced in the unirrigated rainfed coconut gardens is found to be poor and the market value for such copra and desiccated coconut is low. Another noticeable aspect of the nature of production in Tumkur district is the higher percentage of production of tender coconut as compared to the other areas of the country. Further if the small farmers are able to get loans at low rate of interest they will be in a position to overcome the short term financial problems and wait for the coconut to mature instead of producing tender coconut. This would help them to earn higher incomes.

Production Per Acre of Tender, Desiccated Coconut and Copra by Different Size Group of Sample Farmers

The Table-5.3 gives a detailed picture of production per acre of Tender, Desiccated coconut and copra by different caegories of farmers in the irrigated and unirrigated farms.

The productivity per acre or yield per acre in case of small irrigated farmers was observed to be 2999 nuts. Thus the productivity of small farmers in the irrigated sector was found to be very good by any standards. Out of the total production of 2999 coconut, about 967 were consumed in the form of tender coconuts. The percentage of tender coconut in the total produce thus constituted 32.22 percent. The reason for such a large percentage consumption of tender nuts as mentioned earlier is mainly due to the lack

Table 5.3: Production Per Acre of Tender, Desiccated Coconut and Copra by Different Size Group of Farmers, 1994-95

(Nuts in numbers)

Sl. No.	Type of Farmer	Irrigated				Unirrigated			
		Tender Coconut	Desiccated Coconut	Copra	Total Percentage	Tender Coconut	Desiccated Coconut	Copra	Total
1.	Small	967	1199	833	2999	767	923	430	2120
		(32.22)	(40.00)	(27.78)	(100.00)	(36.18)	(43.54)	(20.28)	(100.00)
2.	Medium	334	500	1946	2780	402	410	1218	2030
		(12.00)	(18.00)	(70.00)	(100.00)	(19.82)	(20.18)	(60.00)	(100.00)
3.	Large	118	413	2125	2656	167	304	1493	1964
		(04.45)	(15.55)	(80.00)	(100.00)	(08.52)	(15.48)	(76.00)	(100.00)
	Total	1419	2112	4904	8435	1336	1637	3141	6114

Source: Field Survey.

N.B. : Figures in brackets represent the column percentage to the total, of financial support for the small farmers. The percentage of coconut consumed in the form of desiccated coconut and copra remained low in relation to that of tender coconuts. 1199 coconuts were used as desiccated coconuts and 833 nuts were used in the production of copra. The percentage of copra in the total produce thus stood at 27.78 percent and that of desiccated coconut stood at 40 percent.

The total production by the medium farmers in the irrigated sector was 2780 coconut per acre in the year 1994-95. The plucking of tender coconut was minimal in case of the medium farmers as compared to the small farmers. The production of tender coconut constituted 12 percent of the total. The production of desiccated coconut and copra constituted 18 percent and 70 percent of the total production. The increase in the production of copra is a healthy tendency as the farmers would be in a position to earn higher income.

In case of large farmers in the irrigated sector, the total production was 2656 nuts per acre. Surprisingly the productivity in case of the large size farmers stood at the lowest among the three categories of farmers. Of the total production of 2656 coconuts, the share of tender coconut desiccated coconut and copra were 118, 413 and 2125 nuts respectively. Thus the share of tender coconut in the total production stood at the lowest and that of coconut used for the production of copra stood highest. The large and medium farmers as the figures show were able to withstand the pressure of heavy demand for tender coconut from big cities like Bangalore which is in close proximity. Hence it is clear from the figures available for 1994-95 that the coconut farmers in the Tumkur area were aware of the fact that production of copra and of desiccated coconut are found to be more profitable and are ready to wait till the maturity of coconut rather than plucking them as tender coconut.

The productivity in case of the small unirrigated farms stood at 2120 nuts per acre. Of which 767 nuts were plucked at the tender stage. This constituted 36.18 percent of the total produce. Thus like the irrigated small farmers, unirrigated small farmers also used a major portion of their total produce in the form of tender coconut. The remaining

923 nuts were desiccated coconut and 430 nuts were used in the production of copra. The share of desiccated coconut and copra in the total production stood at 43.54 percent and 20.28 percent per acre. Thus as in the case of small irrigated farmers, the small unirrigated farmers also used comparatively less proportion of their total produce for the production of copra.

Out of the total production of 2030 coconuts by the medium farmers, 402, 410 and 1218 nuts were in the form of tender coconut, desiccated coconut and copra respectively accounting for 19.82, 20.18 and 60 percent respectively. Thus as in the case of irrigated medium farmers, the unirrigated medium farmers also used more number of coconut in the production of copra.

REFERENCES

1. Menon, K.P.V. and Pandalai, K.M.: The Coconut Palm - A monograph, Indian Central Coconut Committee, Ernakulam, 1960, pp 20 - 50.
2. Chikkasubbanna, V. Jayaprasad, K.V. Subiah Thilak and Poonesh, N.M.: Effects of Maturity on the Chemical Composition of Tender Coconut (Cocosnucifera L. Var Arsikere Tale) Water, *Indian Coconut Journal*, 1990, Vol. 20, No. 12, pp 10 - 13.
3. Belfort, R. and Hoyer, A.J.: All about Coconuts, London, St. Catherine Press, 1914, pp 2 - 98.
4. Coconut Planters Manual, Ferguson's All about the Coconut Palm, Colombo, Ceylon, Observer Press, 1923, pp 1 - 120.
5. Crawford, M.: Coconut poonac as a food for livestock, Trop. Agric. Mag. Ceylon, Agric. Soc., 1940, Vol. 44, No. 1, p 168.
6. M. Meerabai, B.K. Jayachandran, M., Abdul Salam and Kunjamma, P. Mathew: Cooking Fuel productivity of coconut trees, Indian Coconut Journal, Vol. XXII, No.8, 1991, pp 13 - 14.
7. Copeiand, E.B.: *The Coconut*, Mac Millan and Co. Ltd., London, 1937, pp 56 - 78.
8. Popenoe, J: *Coconut and Cashew*, North American Tree Nuts, Geneva, N.Y., W.F. Humphrey Press, 1969, pp 1 - 78.
9. George, M.V., K.V. Vijayakumar and Jacob Mathew Trend in area production and productivity of coconut in India, Indian Coconut Journal, 1991, Vol. XXII, Nos. 6 & 7, pp 45 - 48.

CHAPTER 6

MARKETING OF COCONUT

In this Chapter, cost per acre, gross returns, net profits and output-input ratio in the coconut cultivation are anlaysed. Before that, the sales and prices of coconut in two Agricultural Produce Marketing Committees (APMC) namely Ulliyar APMC and Tiptur APMC are studied for a period of ten years to know the trends in marketing of coconut in the Tumkur district. Further marketing of coconut in the different forms in the sample area, has been carried out in case of irrigated and unirrigated holdings.

Processing of coconut in India has not been developed on modern lines. The acvitivies were limited to copra making and oil milling[1]. The present trend is that the prices of various coconut products are determined by the price of coconut oil in different markets. Dependence of coconut industry on one single commodity i.e., coconut oil is causing considerable instability in the coconut cultivation. The price of coconut oil and other coconut products are characterized by unpredictable fluctuations.

METHODS OF MARKETING COCONUTS IN TUMKUR DISTRICT

Tender Coconut

Producers dispose of tender coconut for drinking the coconut water without giving them any sort of dressing. Tender coconut are used for drinking the coconut water which is inside the nut. The husk at one end of the nut, if not already removed, is chopped of by means of a bill-hook and a hole is pearced through which water is taken out[2].

Tender coconuts are disposed immediately after

harvesting. The whole-salers and retailers also do not share tender nuts for more than few days. They are kept loose in a corner of a godown or shop. The interval between the harvesting of the nuts and their consumption rarely exceeds 10 to 12 days[3].

Classification and Grading

There is no regular system of grading tender coconut. The grading is usually done on the basis of the coconut. The bigger nuts fetch higher price as they generally contain more quantity of coconut water.

Distribution

Whole-sale distribution of Tender coconut was hardly found in the sample area as nuts were purchased by hawkers and retailers directly from the owner of the coconut gardens and disposed of at the near by towns and the cities.

Desiccated Coconut

The producers generally dispose off their mature coconut by selling them as husked. Nuts harvested in the monsoon months are some times stored for two or three months. Usually the producers sell the bulk of the coconut in form of husked nuts. Considerable portion of the crop reaches the market and the consumers in the form of husked nuts. The cost of storage varies within wide limits under different conditions, when coconuts are stored is practically nill. When nuts are stored for long periods, for the preparation of dry nuts or edible copra storage involves, handling charges, rental value of that space occupied, interest and losses during storage. All these items are subject to considerable variations in different areas and under different conditions[4].

Classification and Grading of Desiccated Coconut

The main quality factor on the basis which consumer assesses the value of coconut is the quality and quantity of kernel inside. The tender judges the quantity of kernel by the size of the coconut and quality by maturity of the nut.

Markets for Coconut

There are a number of assembling markets in the coconut producing areas to which producers bring their coconut for sale. These markets are held either on government yards or private lands. In most of these markets, coconut is one of the various commodities sold. In some places certain days of the week are exclusively set apart for coconut trading. For instance at ARASIKERE, there is a special market for coconut only on Monday, Wednesday and Saturday during the peak season, (April to September) and Monday and Wednesday during the lean period (Octorber to March). At Tiptur market, auction of coconut takes place on Monday, Wenesday and Saturday.

When coconuts are taken to the market for sale, an octroi duty or toll has often to be paid for entering the market. The head loads or cart after entering the market are generally heaped on the floor and sold by the producers themselves or through the commission agents and the brokers.

Copra

Copra is broadly classified into two categories viz., high quality fit for edible purposes while the second category includes all remaining copra used mainly for the production of oil. This classification is not strictly adhored to. Edible copra is made in the form of balls or cups while milling copra is made in the form of cups only. There are three main classes of copra viz., ball copra, edible and milling copra[5].

Sales Through APMCs in Tumkur District

Large scale marketing of coconut is carried out through the two most important APMC's in Tumkur district namely Ulliyar APMC and Tiptur APMC. These two markets are purposefully selected to know trends in sales and prices of coconut. The data on sales, prices etc were collected for the period of 12 years from 1948-85 to 1995-96 in case of Ulliyar APMC and for the period of 12 years from 1982-83 to 1993-94 in case of Tiptur APMC. The Tiptur and Ulliyar APMC's were selected mainly because the farmers in the sample area bring their coconut produce and sell in these markets. Hence, a study of the arrivals and prices of coconut at these APMC's would through a clear picture of the prices received by the sample farmers. The table 6.1, 6.2, 6.3 and 6.4 show the arrivals and prices of coconut in the Ulliyar and Tiptur APMC's.

The Table-6.1 shows that the wide fluctuations in the sales and prices of copra in the Ulliyar APMC market. During the period 1991-92 and 1993-94, farmers received the highest price for the copra. The price of copra during these years touched all time peak of Rs. 3743 and Rs.4526 per quintal respectively. The lowest price recorded for copra was Rs. 1708 during 1989-90. It is clear that there was a wide fluctuation in the prices of copra during the entire period. Similarly the highest sales took place in the year 1984-85 and the lowest sales in the year 1991-92. In between sales of copra fluctuated very widely. The average sales was found to be 1778 quintals with coefficient of variation 34.98 percent. Similarly the average price of copra estimated to be Rs. 2753 per quintal of copra with co-efficient of variation 30.58 percent.

Table 6.1: Sales and Prices of Copra in Ulliyar APMC Yard, 1984-1996

Sales in Quintals
Price in Rs/ Quintal

Year	Sales	Price per Quintal	Value
1984-85	2760	2531	6985560
1985-86	2717	1757	4773769
1986-87	2144	1779	3814176
1987-88	1957	2717	5317169
1988-89	1427	3658	5219966
1989-90	1930	1708	3296440
1990-91	1849	2277	4210173
1991-92	778	3743	2912054
1992-93	884	4526	4000984
1993-94	995	3174	3158130
1994-95	2020	2544	5138880
1995-96	1870	2626	4910620
Average	1778	2753	
Co-efficient of variation	34.98	30.58	

Source: Agricultural Produce Market Committee, Ulliyar, 1996.

Table 6.2: Sales and Prices of Desiccated Coconut in Ulliyar APMC Yard, 1984-1996

Sales in No. of Coconut
Price in Rs/ Nut

Year	Sales (in numbers)	Price per Coconut	Value (in Rs.)
1984-85	1240200	1.26	1568000
1985-86	856130	1.13	971320
1986-87	2044850	1.87	3830690
1987-88	2696397	1.97	5323866
1988-89	2446520	2.43	5945415
1989-90	2089720	1.39	2874540
1990-91	2400640	1.97	4738180
1991-92	1610500	2.23	3597100
1992-93	1547000	2.25	3481670
1993-94	762000	2.26	1729715
1994-95	1073000	2.36	2541030
1995-96	1217000	3.42	3703220
Average	1665330	2.05	
Co-efficient of variation	97.11	42.93	

Source: Agricultural Produce Market Committee, Ulliyar, 1996.

The Table-6.2 shows the sales and prices of desiccated coconut in Ulliyar APMC market yard during the period 1984-1996. The highest price of Rs. 3.4 per desiccated coconut was received during 1995-96 and the least price of Rs. 1.13 was received during 1985-86. However, one interesting aspect about the prices of desiccated coconut was that it registered a gradual increase throughout the period though there was no uniformity in increase in the price level. It may be noted here that while the price of copra largely depends on the price of coconut oil, the price of desiccated coconut mainly depends on household consumption of desiccated coconut. Due to the imports of coconut oil from foreign countries for industrial purposes the prices of oil are bound to fluctuate and hence the prices of copra. The demand for desiccated coconut is mainly met by the local markets. As the demand for desiccated coconut is on rising trend, the price of desiccated coconut has also increased over the period. The average sales was observed to be 1665330 nuts per year with co-efficient of variation in sales 97.11 percent. Similarly the average price per desiccated coconut was found to be Rs. 2.05 with coefficient variation in price 42.93 percent.

Table 6.3: Sales and Prices of Copra in Tiptur APMC Yard, 1982-1994

Sales in Quintals
Price in Rs/ Quintal

Year	Sales in quintals	Price per Quintal	Value in Rs.
1982-83	219282	1321	289694520
1983-84	120761	2543	307147850
1984-85	107651	2909	313222690
1985-86	209659	1465	301795015
1986-87	249135	1899	473316682
1987-88	149234	2716	405379950
1988-89	130850	2782	364150150
1989-90	204724	2070	423972940
1990-91	275228	2123	584446750
1991-92	204635	3540	724469000
1992-93	185690	2962	735854850
1993-94	210328	3298	693738750
Average	188931	2552	
Co-efficient of variation	8.3	30.49	

The Table-6.3 presents the sales and prices of copra in Tiptur APMC from 1982-83 to 1993-94. The table shows that the highest price of Rs. 3962 per quintal was realized in the year 1992-93 and the least price was realized in 1982-83. In between the price of copra fluctuated very widely.

The sales of copra also showed wide fluctuations. The average sales was observed to be 188931 quintals of copra with co-efficient of variation in sales 8.3 percent. Similarly the average price of copra estimated to be Rs. 2552 per quintal with co-efficient of variation in price 30.49 percent.

Sales and price trends of desiccated coconut showed in Table-6.4 exhibited similar pattern that of the Ulliyar APMC. In the Tiptur APMC, the highest price of desiccated coconut was received during the year 1992-93. During this

Table 6.4: Sales and Prices of Desiccated Coconut in Tiptur APMC Yard, 1982-1994

Sales in No. of Coconuts
Price in Rs/ Coconut

Year	Sales in No. of nuts	Price per Desiccated Coconut	Value in Rs.
1982-83	857341	1.27	1086752
1983-84	789972	2.04	1608790
1984-85	412014	1.78	733385
1985-86	975800	1.38	1342695
1986-87	1399143	2.16	3015927
1987-88	800900	2.62	2096755
1988-89	1545425	2.60	4017335
1989-90	1776090	2.00	3557550
1990-91	1522645	0.51	777473
1991-92	949400	3.60	3402740
1992-93	1823290	4.05	7383700
1993-94	1167700	2.83	3300700
Average	1168060	2.24	
Co-efficient of variation	16.15	0.95	

year the price realized was Rs. 4.05 per nut. The lowest price realized at the Tiptur APMC was during 1990-91 when it hit the bottom of Rs. 0.51 per desiccated coconut.

Marketing of Tender Coconut, Desiccated Coconut and Copra by the Sample Farmers

The estimates of sales of tender coconut, desiccated coconut, copra by the sample farmers are done by taking into coconut the domestic consumption by the farmers. The estimates of sales are presented on the Table-6.5.

Unlike in Kerala State where a major portion of the coconut produced is consumed by the farmers themselves, the consumption of coconut for domestic purposes is negligible in the Tumkur area. The total quantity of tender coconut sold by the irrigated farmers was 119205 nuts during the 1994-95 and the farmer received an average price of Rs. 2 per nut and the total income received by all the farmers by selling tender nut worked out to be Rs.

Table 6.5: Sales of Tender, Desiccated Coconuts, Copra by the Sample Farmers, 1994-95

Variety	Irrigated				Unirrigated			
	Quantity sold	Average price per 1000 NUTS/ quintal	Sales Values (in Rs.)	Average Sales Value per acre received by the farmers (in Rs.)	Quantity sold (in nuts)/ quintals	Average price per 1000 NUTS/ quintal	Total Sales Value (in Rs.)	Average Sales Value per acre received by the farmers (in Rs.)
Tender Coconut (in numbers)	119205	2000	238410 (4.99)	559	54508	2000	109016 (10.66)	713
Desiccated Coconut (in number)	173268	2700	467824 (9.78)	1097	35888	2700	96898 (9.47)	634
Copra (in quintals)	1381.47	2950	4075337 (85.23)	9558	276.88	2950	816796 (79.87)	5343
Total			4781571 (100.00)				1022710 (100.00)	

Source : Field Survey.

N.B.: Figures in brackets represent percentage to the total

238410. In the same way, the income received by the all irrigated farmers by selling desiccated coconut was Rs. 467824. The average price received by the farmers was Rs. 2700 per thousand nuts. The total quantity of copra sold by the irrigated farmers worked out to be 1381.47 quintals. The average price received was Rs. 2950 per quintal and the income received by the farmers worked out to be Rs. 4075337.

In the unirrigated sector total number of tender coconut sold was 54508. The average price received by the farmers was Rs.2 per tender coconut. The total income of the produce received by all the farmers in the year stood at Rs. 109016. The sale of desiccated coconut in the area stood at 35888 nuts and the average price for 1000 nuts stood at Rs. 2700. Income from the sale of desiccated coconut stood at Rs. 96898. A total of 276.88 quintals of copra was sold at an average price of Rs. 2950 per quintal and the total earnigs from the sale of copra in the unirrigated sector stood at Rs. 816796.

In the irrigated sector the earnings from the sale of tender coconut was 4.99 percent of the total earnings from the sale of all three categories of farmers. Further the earnings from sale of desiccated coconut was 9.78 percent of the total and that of copra was 85.23 percent. Thus it is clear that in the sample area the farmers got the highest earnings from the sale of copra.

The total earnings of the farmers in the unirrigated sector from the sale of all the three varieties was just Rs. 1022710 which is very low compared to the irrigated area. Out of the total earnings, the sale of tender coconuts constituted 10.66 percent and that of desiccated coconut and copra constituted 9.47 percent and 79.87 percent respectively.

Marketing of Tender Coconut in the Sample Area

In this section, the marketing of tender coconuts in the sample areas has been discussed, both in the irrigated and unirrigated farmers in all the three types of farmers viz., small, medium and large.

The Table-6.6 shows the marketing of tender coconut by the farmers. The small farmers with irrigation received

Table 6.6: Sales of Tender Coconuts According to Farm Size in the Sample Area, 1994-95

Type of Farmers	Irrigated			Unirrigated		
	Quantity sold (in numbers) (in Rs.)	Average price per nut (in Rs.)	Total Sales Value	Quantity sold (in numbers) (in Rs.)	Average price per nut (in Rs.)	Total Sales Value (in Rs.)
Small	46410	2	92820	22841	2	45682
	(38.93)		(38.93)	(41.90)		(41.90)
Medium	43484	2	86968	18950	2	37900
	(36.48)		(36.48)	(34.77)		(34.77)
Large	29311	2	58622	12717	2	25434
	(24.54)		(24.59)	(23.33)		(23.33)
Total	119205	2	238410	54508	2	109016
	(100.00)		(100.00)	(100.00)		(100.00)

Source: Field Survey
N.B.: Figures in brackets represent percentage to the total

an average price of Rs. 2 per tender coconut. The total income received by the small farmers from the sale amounted to Rs. 92820. As observed in the production analysis, the small farmers had a major share in the total production of tender coconut. The medium size farmers with irrigation sold 43484 tender nuts at an average price of Rs. 2 per nut. The total earning the medium farmers thus amounted to Rs. 86968. The sale of tender coconut by the large scalers amounted to 29311 nuts and their total earnings at Rs. 2 per nut amounted to Rs. 58622. The total sale of tender coconut in the sample area thus worked out to 119205 nuts and at an average rate of Rs. 2 per nut, the total earnings worked out to be Rs. 238410. The share of the small farmers in the total earnings worked out to be 38.93 percent and that of medium and large farmers worked out to be 36.48 percent and 24.59 percent of the total earnings respectively.

In case of unirrigated plantation the sale of tender coconut by the small farmers in the sample area stood at 22841 nuts. The total earnings from the sale of coconut by the small unirrigated farmer thus worked out to be Rs. 45682. The total sale of tender coconut by the medium farmers in the unirrigated sector was 18950 nuts and the total earnings of the medium farmers stood at Rs.37900. The large farmers had a relatively small share in the total sale of tender coconut as compared to the sales of the other two types of farmers. The total sales by the large farmers stood at 12717 nuts and their earnings worked out to be Rs. 25434.

The share of small farmers in the total earning stood in 41.90 percent and that of medium and large farmers stood at 34.77 percent and 23.33 percent respectively. Thus the small farmers marketed large number of tender coconut as compared to medium and large farmers in ease of irrigated as well as unirrigated plantation.

Table 6.7: Sales of Desiccated Coconut According to Farm Size in the Sample Area, 1994-95

Type of Farmers	Irrigated			Unirrigated		
	Quantity sold (in numbers)	Average price per 1000 nuts (in Rs.)	Total Sales Value (in Rs.)	Quantity sold (in numbers) (in Rs.)	Average price per nut (in Rs.)	Total Sales Value (in Rs.)
Small	49616	2700	133963	21488	2700	58018
	(28.84)		(28.64)	(59.88)		(59.88)
Medium	45227	2700	122113	7294	2700	19694
	(26.10)		(26.10)	(20.32)		(20.32)
Large	78425	2700	211748	7106	2700	19186
	(45.26)		(45.26)	(19.8)		(19.80)
Total	173268	2700	467824	35888	2700	96898
	(100.00)		(100.00)	(100.00)		(100.00)

Source: Field Survey
N.B.: Figures in brackets represent percentage to the total

The Table-6.7 shows the sales of desiccated coconut by small, medium and large farmers. The small farmers with irrigated plantation in the sample area had a total sales of 49616 desiccated coconut at an average price of Rs 2700 per one thousand nuts. The total earnings of the small farmers thus worked out to be Rs. 133963. The medium farmers had sold 45227 desiccated coconut and received a total earning of Rs. 122113. The large farmers had sold a major share of their total production in the form of desiccated coconut i.e. 78425 nuts and earned a total income of Rs. 2117.48.

The farmers in the irrigated area thus had a total sale of 173268 desiccated coconut. The share of small, medium and large farmers in the total earnings worked out to be 28.64 percent, 26.10 percent and 45.26 percent of the total.

The small farmers with unirrigated plantation had a total sale of 21488 nuts in the year 1994-95, the total earnings of the small unirrigated farmers from the sale of desiccated coconut accounted to Rs. 58018. In case of medium farmers, the total sale of desiccated coconut was 7294 nuts and a total income of Rs. 19694 was realized. The large farmers had sold 7106 desiccated coconut and their gross income from the sale stood at Rs. 19186.

The farmers with the unirrigated plantation had a total sales of 35888 desiccated nuts and the total income received from the sale was Rs. 96898. The share of the small, medium and large farmers in the total earnings worked out to be 59.88 percent, 20.32 percent and 19.80 percent respectively. Thus it is the small farmers with the unirrigated plantation who had a major share in the total sales of desiccated coconut.

Table 6.8 : Sales of Copra Accoding to Farm Size in the Sample Area, 1994-95

Type of Farmers	Irrigated			Unirrigated		
	Quantity sold (in numbers)	Average price per quintals (in Rs.)	Total Sales Value (in Rs.)	Quantity sold (in quintals) (in Rs.)	Average price per quintals (in Rs.)	Total Sales Value (in Rs.)
Small	66.20 (4.79)	2950	195290 (4.79)	18.72	2950	55224 (6.76)
Medium	426.20 (30.85)	2950	1257290 (30.85)	86.10	2950	253995 (31.10)
Large	889.07 (64.36)	2950	2622757 (64.36)	172.06	2950	507577 (62.14)
Total	1381.47 (100.00)	2950	4075337 (100.00)		2950	816796 (100.0)

Source: Field Survey
N.B.: Figures in brackets represent percentage to the total

It is very important to know the total sales of copra by the different farms as the sale of copra provides the farmers reasonably good income. One important factor about copra prices is that it fluctuates with the price of coconut oil. In the year 1994-95, the net sale of copra by the small irrigated farmers amounted to 66.20 quintals at an average price of Rs. 2950 per quintal, and the earnings of the small farmers amounted to Rs. 195290. The medium farmers had sold an output of 426.20 quintals of copra and earned a total income of Rs. 1257290. The large farmers as compared to the other two categories of farmers, were the highest producers of copra, their total sales of copra stood at 889.07 quintals and earned an income of Rs. 2622757.

The total production of copra by all categories of farmers in the irrigated sector stood at 1381.48 quintals and the total sales value amounted to Rs. 4075337. The share of the small, medium and large farmers in the total earnings stood at 4.79 percent, 30.85 percent and 64.36 percent respectively. Thus the large farmers had a lion share in the total earnings realized by the sale of copra.

The sale of copra by the small unirrigated farmers in the sample area was just 18.72 quintals. At the market price of Rs. 2950 per quintal, the small farmers received Rs. 55224. The medium farmers sold 86.10 quintals of copra and their earnings from the sale was Rs. 253995. Again the large farmers who produced the bulk of the copra in the unirrigated sector, sold 172.06 quintals for which they received an income of Rs. 507577.

The total sale of the copra by the farmers in the unirrigated sector was 276.88 quintals and received a total income Rs. 316796. The share of large farmer was 62.14 percent and that of medium and small farmers was 31.10 percent and 6.76 percent respectively.

Sales of Tender, Desiccated Coconut and Copra Per Acre According to Farm Size

From the data collected from the sample farmers, the per acre sales and income generated from such sales have been derived and presented in the Table-6.9 and 6.10. A study of this sort will help us to know the feasibility of growing coconut plantation in the district as it can be an indicative of the income generated from the cultivation of coconut by the farmers of this area. Farmers who intend to venture into the coconut farming can have a clear picture of their returns before hand from such an analysis. Sales and income generated per acre by the farmers according to farm size coming under the irrigated plantation are presented in the Table-6.9. It is clear that the total sales of tender coconuts in the irrigated area amounted to 1418 nuts per acre and income generated to the farmers is found to be Rs. 2836 pre acre. The small farmers market more nuts in the form of tender coconuts

Table 6.9: Sales of Tender, Desiccated Coconut and Copra Per Acre According to Farm Size 1994-95 (Irrigated Farms)

Type of Farmers	Tender Coconut		Desiccated Coconut		Copra		Total Sales Value Per Acre (in Rs.)
	Sales Per Acre (in numbers)	Sales Value Per Acre (in Rs.)	Sales Per Acre (in numbers)	Sales Value Per Acre (in Rs.)	Sales Per Acre (in numbers)	Sales Value Per Acre (in Rs.)	
Small	966	1932 (21.97)	1033	2789 (31.72)	1.38	4071 (46.3)	8792 (100.00)
Medium	334	668 (5.94)	347	937 (8.33)	3.27	9647 (85.74)	11252 (100.00)
Large	118	236 (2.03)	316	853 (7.32)	3.58	10561 (90.65)	11650 (100.00)
Total	1418	2836	1696	4579	8.23	24279	31694

Source: Field Survey

N.B.: Figures in brackets represent percentage to the total

and as a result the per acre revenue from the sale of tender coconut is highest. The small farmers in the sample area sold 966 tender coconuts per acre on an average and their income from the sale of tender coconuts stood at Rs. 1932 per acre. This is very high as compared to the income generated to medium and large farmers by selling tender coconuts. Average revenue earned by the medium and large farmers by sale of tender coconut stood at Rs. 668 per acre Rs. 236 per acre respectively. The small farmers got a total of Rs. 8792 per acre from the sale of various farms of coconuts and the income generated by the sale of tender coconut is found to be Rs. 1932. This forms 21.97 percent of the total income. In case of medium and large farmers, the per acre income by selling all forms of coconuts stood at Rs. 11252 and Rs. 11650 constituting at 5.94 percent and 2.03 percent respectively.

Average per acre sale of desiccated coconut in case of the small farmers as seen from the total stood at 1033 nuts and the income generated to farmers stood at Rs. 2789 per acre. The income received by the sale of desiccated coconuts thus formed 31.72 percent of the total income generated to small farmers. Whereas in case of the medium farmers, average sales per acre of desiccated coconut stood at 347 nuts and income generated from the sale stood at Rs. 937 per acre accounting for 8.33 percent of the total income. In case of large farmers income per acre from the sale of desiccated coconut stood at Rs. 853 constituting 7.32 percent of their total income.

Average sale of copra by the small farmers was 1.38 quintals per acre and the average income derived by the sale of copra was found to be Rs. 4071 per acre which forms 46.3 percent of the total earnings of the small farmers. In comparison to this, the medium and large farmers sold 3.27 and 3.58 quintals of copra per acre respectively. The income earned by the medium farmers from the sale of copra was Rs. 9647 per acre accounting 85.74 percent of their total income. Such income in case of large farmers stood at Rs. 10561 constituting 90.65 percent of their total income. Thus the large and medium farmers derived more income by selling copra.

Income earned by the unirrigated farmers also followed

Table 6.10: Sales of Tender, Desiccated Coconut and Copra Per Acre According to Farm Size 1994-95 (Unirrigated Farms

Type of Farmers	Tender Coconut		Desiccated Coconut		Copra		Total Sales Value Per Acre (in Rs.)
	Sales Per Acre (in numbers)	Sales Value Per Acre (in Rs.)	Sales Per Acre (in numbers)	Sales Value Per Acre (in Rs.)	Sales Per Acre (in numbers)	Sales Value Per Acre (in Rs.)	
Small	767	1534 (28.7)	722	1949 (36.48)	0.63	1859 (34.80)	5342 (100.00)
Medium	402	804 (12.14)	155	419 (6.33)	1.83	5399 (81.53)	6622 (100.00)
Large	167	334 (4.60)	94	254 (3.50)	2.26	6667 (91.90)	7255 (100.00)
Total	1336	2672	971	2622	4.72	13925	19219

Source: Field Survey

N.B.: Figures in brackets represent percentage to the total

similar pattern as that of the irrigated farmers. The small farmers in the unirrigated sector earned Rs. 1534 per acre from the sale of tender coconut, Rs. 1949 per acre from the sale of desiccated coconut and Rs. 1859 from the sale of copra. Thus small farmers derived a total income of Rs. 5342 per acre of coconut plantation. The earnings of small farmers constituted 28.7 percent from the sale of tender coconut, 36.48 percent form the sale of desiccated coconut and 34.80 percent from the sale of copra. The medium and the large farmers on an average sold 402 and 167 tender nuts per acre and earned an average revenue of Rs. 804 and 334 per acre constituting 12.14 percent and 4.60 percent of their total income respectively.

The earnings of medium farmers constituted 12.14 percent from the sale of tender coconut, 6.33 percent from the sale of copra. Similarly the total earnings Rs. 7255 per acre in case of large farmers constituted 4.6 percent from the sale of tender coconut, 3.5 percent from the sale of desiccated coconut and as high as 91.90 percent from the sale of copra.

Income from the By-products of Coconuts

Coconut is often referred to as the Kalpa Vruksha (tree of heaven) for the multiple uses that it brings to mankind. Each part of the coconut tree is useful and there are many industries based on coconut which provide employment to large section of the population. Hence an attempt is made to concentrate on raw by-products like Husks, Hardshell, Leaves etc., sold at the farm level.

The Table-6.11 shows the income earned by the farmers from the sale of by-products. On an average small farmers earned Rs. 150.33 per acre of which the income received from the sale of husk was Rs. 20.20. This constituted 13.44 percentage of the total earnings. Similarly they earned Rs. 48.93 and Rs. 81.20 respectively from the sale of hardshell and leaves constituting 32.55 and 54.01 percent of the total income respectively.

In case of the medium irrigated farmers the total income from the sale of by-products was Rs. 227.87 per acre and the share of husk, hardshell and leaves constituted 31.28, 40.46 and 28.26 percent respectively. The large

Table 6.11: Income From By-products of Coconut Per Acre According to Farm Size, 1994-95

(in Rs.)

By-product	Farm Size							
	Irrigated				Unirrigated			
	Small	Medium	Large	Total	Small	Medium	Large	Total
Husks	20.20 (13.44)	71.27 (31.28)	79.98 (34.34)	171.45 (28.05)	18.30 (14.21)	62.70 (32.83)	69.28 (34.83)	150.28 (28.83)
Hardshell	48.93 (32.55)	92.20 (40.46)	109.60 (47.05)	250.73 (41.03)	32.40 (25.16)	76.20 (39.90)	92.10 (45.70)	200.70 (38.50)
Leaves	81.20 (54.01)	64.40 (28.26)	43.35 (18.61)	188.95 (30.92)	78.10 (60.64)	52.10 (27.28)	40.15 (19.92)	170.35 (32.68)
Total	150.33 (100.00)	227.87 (100.00)	232.93 (100.00)	611.13 (100.00)	128.80 (100.00)	191.00 (100.00)	201.53 (100.00)	521.33 (100.00)

Source: Field Survey

N.B.: Figures in brackets represent percentage to the total

irrigated farmers had an average income of Rs.232.93 per acre from the sale of by-products, in which the contribution of husk, hardshell and leaves were 34.34, 47.05, and 18.61 percent respectively.

In an unirrigated plantation, the small farmers earned an average income of Rs. 128.80 per acre in which the shares of husk, hardshell and leaves were 14.21, 25.16 and 60.64 percent respectively. In case of the medium unirrigated farmers, the total earnings from the sale of by-products stood at Rs. 191 per acre and the share of husk, hardshell and leaves was 32.83, 39.90 and 27.28 percent respectively. Large scale farmers had an average income of 201.53 per acre from the sale of by-products in which husk, hardshell and leaves constituted 34.38, 45.70 and 19.92 percent respectively.

Cost, Gross Returns, Net Profit and Output-Input Ratio:

The cost, Gross returns, net profit per acre and output-input ratio in coconut cultivation in the irrigated and unirrigated plantation are presented in the Table-6.12.

In case irrigated plantation, the small farmers have obtained the highest yield of coconut i.e. 2999 nuts per acre and derived gross returns of Rs. 8942. The cost of production was Rs. 4641 per acre. Thus on an average a small farmer derived net income of Rs. 4301 per acre of coconut plantation. The output-input ratio thus stood at 1.93. The medium farmers produced 2780 nuts per acre and derived gross returns of Rs. 11480. The cost incurred during the year was Rs. 4367 per acre and as a result the medium size farmer was able to earn a net profit of Rs. 7113 per acre. The output-input ratio in case of the medium farmers was found to be 2.63. The large farmers produced 2656 coconuts per acre during the year and obtained gross returns of Rs. 11883. The cost during the year was Rs. 4254 per acre and as a result on an average the large farmer derived a net profit of Rs. 7629 per acre. The output-input ratio thus was found to be 2.79 in case of large farmers.

It may be observed here that though the small farmer was able to produce more per unit area than the other two categories, his net profit and output-input ratio were found

Table 6.12: Cost, Gross Returns, Net Profit and Output-Input Ratio in Coconut Cultivation by the Sample Farmers

Sl. No.	Particulars	Farm Size							
		Irrigated				Unirrigated			
		Small	Medium	Large	Total	Small	Medium	Large	Total
1.	Yield per acre (No. of nuts)	2999	2780	2656	2812	2120	2030	1964	2038
2.	Gross returns per acre (in Rs.)	8942	11480	11883	10768	5471	6813	7457	6580
3.	Cost per acre (in Rs.)	4641	4367	4254	4420	3356	3199	3072	3209
4.	Net Profit per acre (in Rs.)	4301	7113	7629	6348	2115	3614	4385	3371
5.	Output-Input Ratio (returns per rupee of investment)	1.93	2.63	2.79	2.44	1.63	2.13	2.42	2.05

Source: Field Survey

N.B.: Figures in brackets represent percentage to the total

to be low as compared to other two categories. This is mainly due to the sale of large number of tender coconut by the small farmers as compared to other two categories.

Further from the table it is clear that the cost of cultivation for all the three categories varies widely with the small farmers incurring high cost as compared to other two categories. This is mainly due to economics of scale applicable to large and medium farmers.

In case of unirrigated plantation, the small farmers produced on average of 2120 nuts per acre and obtained gross returns of Rs. 5471 per acre. The cost of cultivation stood at Rs. 3356 per acre. Thus derived a net profit of Rs. 2115. The output-input ratio worked out to be 1.63. The medium farmers had an average production of 2030 nuts per acre and derived gross returns of Rs. 6813 per acre whereas the cost incurred was Rs. 3199 per acre. Thus net profit earned was 3614 per acre. The output-input ratio stood at 2.13. Similarly, the large farmers had an average production of 1964 nuts per acre and the gross returns amounted to Rs. 7457 per acre and the cost involved was 3072 per acre. Thus the net profit earned by the large farmers amounted to Rs. 4385 per acre. The output-input ratio worked out to be 2.42. Thus for a rupee investment the large farmers obtained high returns both in case of irrigated and unirrigated coconut plantation.

On the whole the performance of a farmer in the irrigated plantation was 2812 nuts per acre with average gross returns of Rs. 10768 per acre. The average per acre cost amounted to Rs. 4420. Thus average net profit of a farmer was observed to be Rs. 6348 per acre. The output-input ratio is found to be 2.54 indicating coconut farming is a profitable enterprise.

In case of the unirrigated plantation the overall performance a farmer was 2038 nuts per acre with average gross returns of Rs. 6580 per acre. The average per acre cost was Rs. 3209. Thus, on an average, a farmer was able to drive a net profit of Rs. 3371 per acre. The output-input ratio was found to be 2.05. Thus it is clear that the irrigated sector out weighs the unirrigated sector in all the areas. The only consolation in the unirrigated sector is that of a lower cost of cultivation. This however is due to the non application of fertilizers. From the analysis, it is clear that irrigation is one major factor that plays an important role in the coconut plantation and a higher productivity can be attained with provision of water to coconut plantation. Thus raising of coconut plantation is profitable in Tumkur district and particularly it is highly remunerative in case of irrigated plantation.

REFERENCES

1. Prafulla K. Das : Price behaviour of coconut oil in relation to major oils in India, *Journal of Plantation Crops*, Vol. 18, No.2, 1991, pp. 376 - 382.
2. Chatterjee, R.K. and Ghose, S: A study of tender nut market of Calcutta, *Indian Coconut Journal*, Vol. 21, No.7 & 8, 1990, pp. 18 - 21.
3. Hanz Kaunitz and Conrado S. Daynt: *Coconut oil consumption and coronary heart disease*, Vol. XXV, No.8, 1994, pp. 13 - 15.
4. Das, P.K.: Movement of whole sale prior of coconut copra and coconut oil in Kerala during the last two and half decades, *Journal of Plantation Crops*, Vol. 14, No. 2, 1986, pp. 105 - 114.
5. Kurup, P.A. and Rajmohan, T.: *Consumption of coconut oil and coconut kernel and Incidence of Atherosclerosis*, Vol. XXV, No.3, 1994, pp. 2 - 16.

CHAPTER 7

SUMMARY AND CONCLUSIONS

A brief summary of the findings derived in the previous chapters are presented here to draw appropriate conclusions for the Economics of coconut plantation.

SUMMARY OF THE FINDINGS

The coconut palm is a versatile tree crop. No other tree crop grown in India can match coconut palm in its versatility. It provides nutritious food and refreshing drink, oil for edible and non-edible uses, fibre of commercial value, shell for fuel and industrial uses, alcoholic beverage, lumber and variety of miscellaneous products for use as domestic fuel. The palm is amenable to both plantation and homestead management. It tolerates other crops grown in the same holdings and thus adjusts itself either as a major or minor crop. While responding favourably to scientific management, the palm also tolerates negligent farming to a certain extent. Thus it can adopt to the divergent farming situations and management practices that are prevalent in the different agro-climatic regions.

Plantation crops are very important for the national economy from the view point of their vast employment potential, income generation, cxport and import substitution. Among these, coconut palm is a versatile plant which is most valuable to the small farmers in the tropical world. Almost every part of this palm is used for the daily needs of the people and it is rightly described as "Kalpavruksha".

Coconut in India is a crop of great importance. It is a crop with many uses. It is a source of food, drink and shelter to the humanity. Coconut is known as

"Kalpavruksha" or the tree of heaven in our country due to advantages and various uses the palm offers. It is valued both as a food crop and an oil seed. India ranks third in the world in coconut production, next to Philippines and Indonesia.

Copra and coconut oil are the two traditional commodities in the domestic markets. Coconut oil commands a unique position as a premium priced oil for both edible as well as non-edible uses and six percent of the vegetable oil production in the country is accounted by coconut oil and is cherished by Keralites as a cooking medium.

More than to million people depend directly or indirectly on the crop for their livelihood by its cultivation-processing, trade and industrial activities. The cost industry which provides direct employment to more than 4 lakh workers, derives its raw material from coconut. Export of coir and coir products earns foreign exchange to the tune of Rs. 100 crores every year. In the recent years industrial units based on coconut kernel and coconut shell have come into existence creating wide employment opportunity to a sizable section of the population and export opportunity.

Coconut is not grown in all the states of India, but is confined to coastal belts and certain interior tracks where the agro climatic conditions favour its growth. It is grown continuously in the major growing states of Kerala and in island groups such as Lakshadweep, Andaman and Nicobar Island and Kasaikal in union territory of Pondicherry. In other states it is confined to certain pockets accounting small area in each state. The four major coconut growing states viz., Kerala, Tamil Nadu, Karnataka and Andhra Pradesh together account for more than 91 percent of area under coconut in India. The small state of Kerala, with 55.8 percent of the area accounts for 41.9 percent of the production of coconut in India in 1991-92. Karnataka State stands at the third place both in terms of area under coconut and production in the country.

The present study is carried out to understand the economics of coconut plantation by examining a case study of Tumkur District in Karnataka. The large scale cultivation in Tumkur district of coconut is mainly concentrated in Tiptur and Chiknayakanahalli talukas, occupying an area of 16384 hectares in Tiptur forming about 25.21 percent of the total area under coconut in the district. Therefore, Tiptur and Chiknayakanahalli talukas were purposely selected for the study. Two villages were selected at random from each taluka. The names of the selected villages are i) Madenure, ii) Biligere from Tiptur taluka and iii) Kenkere, iv) Thimlapura from Chiknayakanahalli taluka. The farmers of the sample villages were divided into three groups, based on the size of their land holdings, namely, small medium and large. The list of farmers with the land holdings owned by them was obtained from the records available with the Village Accountants of the respective villages. In all 120 sample farmers from the four selected villages were chosen for detailed investigation on various aspects of cost of cultivation, production, productivity of coconut garden, income derived, marketing of coconut etc. For evaluating the objectives of the study necessary primary data were obtained from the selected farmers through personal interview method with the help of pre-tested and structured schedule. The primary data were collected for the agricultural year 1994-95. The study has been carried out with the following objectives.

(i) to estimate the trends in the area, production and productivity of coconut crop in Tumkur District also in Karnataka

(ii) to estimate the average cost of cultivation of coconut, production, productivity, income received and output-input ratio in the cultivation of coconut plantation in Tumkur District.

(iii) to study the economic viability of raising of coconut plantation in Tumkur District.

The following hypotheses have been tested in the study:

(i) Area, production and productivity of coconut plantation have increased significantly in the Tumkur district and also in Karnataka.

(ii) Coconut plantation is profitable in the Tumkur District.

(iii) Big farmers are benefited more by coconut plantation as compared to small and medium farmers.

The compound growth rates of area, production and productivity of coconut for Karnataka are found to be 3.06 percent, 3.14 percent and 0.01 percent respectively for the period 1980-1994. Growth rate of area, production and productivity at the Tumkur district level are estimated to be 2.35 percent, 3.51 percent and 1.25 percent respectively for the period 1984-85 to 1995-96. The compound growth rates of area in case of major coconut growing districts like Tumkur, Hassan, Chitradurga, Chikmagalore are estimated to be 6.44 percent, 1.93 percent, 4.95 percent 2.09 percent, respectively for the period 1980-81 to 1993-94. The compound growth rates of production in case of Tumkur, Hassan, Chitradurga and Chikmagalore are estimated to be 12.77 percent, 1.98 percent 4.28 prcent 2.16 percent respectively. The growth rate production of coconut is found to be very impressive in Tumkur district. The compound growth rates of impressive in Tumkur district. The compound growth rates of productivity in these districts; Tumkur, Hassan, Chitradurga and Chikmagalore are estimated to be 5.95 percent, 9.75 percent and -0.01 percent and -0.07 percent respectively for the period 1980-81 to 1993-94. While Chitradurga and Chickmagalore districts have registered negative growth rates, Tumkur and Hassan have witnessed good progress in improving productivity.

The area under coconut in major coconut growing states in India showed an impressive growth during the period 1955-56 to 1970-71, but the growth rate is slacked in the seventies and early eighties. It is surprising to note that actually there was reduction in production of coconut in Kerala, which resulted in lower growth rate in all India level. Even in Karnataka there was no considerable increase during the fifties but a steady increase in the average production was noticed during the seventies and eighties. The only exception to this general trend is in Andhra Pradesh where there was only marginal changes in area during the period 1950-51, but showed a slow but steady increase thereafter. The total production of coconut during 1950-51 was only 3582 million nuts which rose to

9283 million nuts during 1989-90 recording an increase of 157 percent over a period of 40 years. It is interesting to note that there was a steep rise in production of coconut in all the states during the period 1985-1990. In Karnataka the production increased upto 1970-71 and then there was declining trend till 1980-81. As a result of well distributed rainfall from 1984-85 onwards, the production of coconut in Andhra Pradesh, Tamil Nadu and Kerala increased considerably which boosted the all India production to the level of 9283.4 million nuts during 1989-90. An Andhra Pradesh, the production of coconut fluctuated and showed a declining trend till 1985-86 but showed a steep rise thereafter. The production of 195.8 million nuts recorded during 1985-86 which reached 654.7 million nuts during 1989-90. The low level of production in Andhra Pradesh for 1970-71 to 1985-86 was mainly due to the frequent cyclones and the recurring droughts in coconut growing areas. In Tamil Nadu, the production was round 400 million nuts during sixties. During seventies and eighties the production increased steadily with a steep increase during last four years. In Karnataka the total production of coconut was slowly increasing throughout the four decades except during the first half of sixties. Productivity of coconut in major coconut growing states in India shows that the average productivity in India during 1950-51 was 5759 nuts per hectare which increased to 6532 nuts during 1955-56. Thereafter productivity was found to be declining steadily throughout except during last four years. The declining trend in all India productivity was mainly due to the declining trend in Kerala. During 1950-51, Kerala produced 2026 million nuts accounting for 57 percent in the national production which slipped down to 47 percent during 1989-90 though the actual production increased to 4394 million nuts during 1989-90. In Kerala, the average productivity of 6917 nuts per hectare during 1955-56 was highest and then decreased to 5617 nuts during 1956-66 and to 4964, 4792 nuts during 1975-76 and 1985-86 respectively. The existence of larger areas under rainfed conditions resulted in the lower productivity in Kerala. By providing irrigation facilities for coconut gardens particularly in the northern districts of Kerala where the dry spell extends to 5-6 months, the productivity of palms can be enhanced considerably. In Karnataka the productivity per hectare was relatively low during the fifties and sixties with a dip during 1965-66 and reached the all India level during seventies and remained without much fluctuations. In Tamil Nadu the productivity per hectare was always high, though fluctuating widely. The average productivity was almost double than that of Kerala. It is interesting to note that the high density of palms, which is about 319 palms per hectare. The corresponding figures of Kerala and Karnataka are 229 and 112, respectively. Though average yield per palm in Karnataka is 54 nuts, the yield per hectare is low because of very low palm density. Whereas in Tamil Nadu with a low average yield of 44 nuts per palm, the productivity is found to be almost double than that of Kerala as well as the country as a whole.

Considering districtwise area, production and productivity of coconut in Karnataka during 1980-81, Hassan district was found to be dominant in areawise, Chitradurga district dominant in productionwise. But drastic change could be seen in the area, production and yield after 1985. Tumkur district out did other districts. For instance during 1989-90 the area under coconut cultivation was 53 thousand hectares and production stood at 352.3 million nuts with an yield rate of 6647 nuts per hectare. And this trend has continued thereafter. It could be interesting to note the growth trend in area cultivated, production and productivity at national, state and district levels. The area expansion under coconut at the national level has shown better performance than that of state and district levels. At the national level the area under coconut has increased by 35.37 percent in 1994-95 over the base year 1985-86. At the state and Tumkur district levels, the area under coconut has increased by 20.62 percent and 19.35 percent in 1994-95 over the base year 1985-86. At the national level and district level production has increased by 35-39 percent and 32.53 percent in 1994-95 over the base year 1985-86 respectively. At the state level production has increased by only 21.0 percent during the above period. However, it is the Tumkur district which as excelled the national and state level performance in terms of productivity. The productivity has increased by 16.35

percent in Tumkur district whereas at the state level the productivity has increased by only 0.6 percent and at the national level, productivity has remained stagnant and no change has taken place in the productivity. It can ultimately be inferred that the position of Tumkur district in the coconut economy in terms area production and productivity is far better than that of the state and national levels. This shows the importance of coconut economy in Tumkur district.

The primary objective of this study is to investigate the feasibility of raising coconut plantation in Karnataka in general and in Tumkur district in particular. In this regard, the study has attempted to estimate the cost of cultivation of coconut plantation, production, productivity of coconut, gross returns, net income, and output-input ratio with the help of primary data.

Cost of production during the establishment period is found to be very high and the farmers need to spend large amount of money for 6 to 7 years without having any returns from the plantation. The study revealed that the farmers in the Tumkur district are hesitant to venture into coconut farming due to the initial investment, uncertainty about the yield after the establishment period and the ignorance about the advantages of coconut plantation.

Total cost per acre during the establishment period in case of irrigated small, medium and large farmers worked out to be Rs. 21707, Rs. 21067 and Rs. 20885 respectively. Out of the total cost, material cost (fertilizer and compost), labour and irrigation cost were found to be estimated at 12.94 percent, 23.08 percent and 50.75 percent respectively in case of small farmers. In case of medium farmers fertilizer and compost, labour and irrigation costs were found to be 22.95 percent, 32.28 percent and 50.72 percent respectively. Similarly, in case of large farmers, material (fertilizer and compost), labour and irrigation costs were estimated at 12.83 percent, 20.86 percent and 52 percent respectively during 7 year establishment period.

The total cost per acre in the first year of economic period in case of small, medium and large (irrigated) farmers worked out to be Rs. 4641, Rs. 4367 and Rs. 4254 respectively. Out of the total cost, material (fertilizer and compost), labour and irrigation costs were found to be estimated at 8.23 percent, 20.69 percent and 23.27 percent respectively in case of small farmers. In case of medium farmers, material cost (fertilizer and compost), labour and irrigation costs were found to be 8.06 percent, 20.61 percent and 21.98 percent respectively. Similarly material cost (fertilizer and compost), labour and irrigation costs were found to be estimated at 6.75 percent, 20.45 percent and 22.57 percent respectively in case of large farmers.

The total cost per acre during establishment period (unirrigated) worked out to be Rs. 16638, Rs. 15375 and Rs. 14874 respectively. Out of the total cost, material cost (fertilizer and compost), labour and irrigation costs were estimated at 6.92 percent, 27.62 percent and 48.32 percent respectively in case of small farmers. In case of medium farmers compost and fertilizer, labour and irrigation costs accounted for 11.60 percent, 26.58 percent and 48.20 percent respectively. In case of large farmers, fertilizer and manure, labour and irrigation costs accounted for 6.49 percent, 26.55 percent and 47.96 percent respectively.

The total cost per acre in the first year of economic period in case of unirrigated farms for small, medium and large farmers worked out to be Rs. 3356, Rs. 3199 and Rs. 3936 respectively. Out of this total cost, material (fertilizer and compost), labour and irrigation costs for small farmers, were 5.60, 17.28 and 26.82 respectively. In case of medium farmers, material (fertilizer and compost), labour and irrigation costs were estimated at 4.88 pecent, 19.07 percent, and 27.20 percent respectively. In case of large farmers material (fertilizer and compost), labour and irrigation costs were estimated at 4.68 percent, 19.86 percent and 26.37 percent respectively.

Irrigation is observed to be very expensive in case of small and medium size farmers. Major part of the expenditure of coconut production is on irrigation. The farmers in the Tumkur area can reduce cost by adopting soil conservation methods like husk barrial. The study also reveals that a major investment goes for the application of chemical fertilizers. The prices of chemical fertilizers go on increasing from time to time and the expenditure on chemical fertilizers will always be on the increasing trend. Hence, use of compost and judicious use of chemical fertilizers is essential so as to develop the low cost management in the production of coconut.

The yield per acre of coconut in case of the small farmers was high as compared to that of the large and medium size farmers in both irrigated and unirrigated plantation. This is inspite of the fact large size farming has various advantages. The small farms of the Tumkur district are found to be more efficient than the medium and large farms in the production of coconut.

The production in the irrigated plantation is observed to be higher than that of the production in the unirrigated plantation. This proves that the productivity of coconut palms can be directly attributed to the availability of water.

The average yield of nuts per acre or the productivity of coconut in Tumkur is higher than the national average and also that of many traditional coconut producing states. This, in addition to the low cost of cultivation proves that coconut cultivation can be done profitably in Tumkur as well as in Karnataka.

The small farmers of the study area produced more of tender nuts as compared to the medium and large farmers. The small farmers had a major share in the total production of tender nuts. The small farmers did not give much attention to the production of copra and desiccated coconut due to their urgent need for finance and their inability to wait till the maturity of coconut. Hence there is a need for financial institutions that can help the farmers so that distress sales can be avoided.

Like in other coconut growing areas, the medium and large size coconut growers of the sample area are well aware of the fact that the production of desiccated coconut and copra can bring large profits to them because of high prices. As a result, their production was found to be constituted mainly desiccated coconut and copra.

It may be observed here that though the small irrigated and unirrigated farmers were able to produce more per unit area than the other two categories the net profit and output-input ratios in case of small farmers were found to be less than other two categories. This is mainly due to the sale of large number of tender coconut by the small farmers as compared to other two categories.

The performance in the irrigated sector was found to be superior to the unirrigated sector in all the areas. The only consolation in the unirrigated sector is that of a low cost of cultivation and this is mainly due to the non-application of fertilizers. From the analysis, it is clear that irrigation is one major factor that plays an important role in the coconut plantation and a highest productivity can be attained when coconut plantations are provided with water. Thus raising of coconut plantation was found to be highly profitable in Tumkur district in case of irrigated plantation. It is also found that the production of coconut can also be carried out profitably even in the unirrigated areas of Tumkur district without incurring heavy cost.

The study on marketing reveals that there are wide fluctuations in the prices of coconut and related items. This is mainly due to the fluctuation in the price of coconut oil.

The study further reveals that there are no major coconut related industries in the near vicinity of the sample area. The coir manufacturing units, soap manufacturing units etc., which make use coconut as a raw material are not found in the vicinity of the sample area. The marketing of coconut is largely done in the raw form in the absence of cottage industries like soap, coir and carpet manufacturing units. As a result, farmers get low prices and the new farmers are hesitating to enter into the coconut plantation.

The sale of coconut is mainly concentrated in the form of tender coconut, desiccated coconut and copra. The sale in the advanced form like sale of coconut oil, coconut vinegar etc. is not done by the farmers.

A careful examination of the earnings of the coconut farmers in the small, medium and large groups both in the irrigated and unirrigated plantation shows that the farmers are in a position to earn a good income from the coconut plantation. Thus, coconut plantation is economically viable to the farmers of the Tumkur district which provides better income and employment to a large section of the population.

CONCLUSIONS

On the basis of the results of the present study the following conclusions are drawn:

1. The estimates of growth rates of area, production and productivity of coconut indicate that though there was considerable expansion in area under coconut, and increase in production, there is a vast scope for increasing the productivity levels in the Tumkur district as well as in Karnataka State. For this, one of the basic requirements is the promotion of irrigation facilities. The response of coconut to irrigation is found to be significant, the provision of irrigation facilities to coconut plantation would go a long way in increasing the production and as well as productivity in the district/ state. Efforts should be made to create irrigation in the district so that new area under coconut plantation with irrigation facilities would boost production as well as productivity.
2. In addition to irrigation, chemical fertilizers, use of compost and application of pesticides are very important in increasing the productivity of coconut gardens. Therefore efforts should be made to conduct large number of fertilizer experiments in the farmers garden covering different soil types, under rainfed and irrigated conditions. It is also important to fix up fertilizer schedules for pre-bearing and bearing palms in irrigated and unirrigated plantations.
3. In the establishment of coconut gardens, the first and foremost thing is raising quality seedlings/ procuring seedlings from a well known orchard. Efforts must be made to raise and distribute quality seedlings at subsidized rates particularly to small farmers which will ensure not only cent percent survivability but also will help to increase production and productivity of palms.
4. Cost of cultivation of coconut can still be reduced in the Tumkur district as well as in other parts of the

country by adoption of soil conservation methods which help to increase moisture content of the soil and hence reduces the cost of irrigation. Again the small farmers can reduce their cost by resorting to group management. Therefore, the farmers should be encouraged and helped to adopt soil conservation methods.

5. The drip irrigation techniques developed for coconut gardens supplies the daily water need of 32 litres/ palm in dry months at four dripping points located at one metre distance from the hole around the palm. The water is allowed to drip at about 30 cm below the soil surface at the rate of 2 litres/ hour. This eliminates loss of nutrients by leaching. There is about 40 percent saving of water than in basin system of irrigation. There is no weed growth, since surface remains dry thus appreciably reducing the cost of weeding. The farmers should be encouraged by providing sufficient technical knowledge and required credit so as to adopt drip irrigation technique for coconut plantation which will help to reduce the cost of cultivation to a great extent.

6. The development of mixed farming and multiple cropping systems in the coconut garden lands is also note worthy as compared to a monocrop of coconut. Under mixed farming, the interspaces in coconut gardens are planted with fodder grasses and legumes, black pepper, banana or other fruit trees. Fodder grasses and legumes grown in one hectare of coconut garden under irrigation could maintain 4 to 5 milch animals and provides full employment to a medium size farm family. And the cow dung when cycled trough a biogas plant produces gas adequate to meet the lighting and cooking needs of the farming family. The recycled dung thereafter can be applied to the palms and grass as manure. Under experimental conditions, the present net income per hectare of coconut garden under mixed farming with irrigation could be increased as much as 300 percent. The farmers should be given sufficient guidance and financial support so as to adopt mixed farming and

multiple cropping systems in the coconut garden lands.

7. Organic manure, green manure and use of oil cakes, these three types of organic farming in coconut not only ensures continuous supply of nutrients to the coconut, but also improves the physical characteristics of soil and increases the population of beneficial micro organisms present in the soil. And recently proved that these manures can be used for the control of pests and diseases. Therefore concerted efforts should be undertaken to use these locally available manures for the benefit of small and marginal farmers of our country.

8. Unfortunately Research and Development efforts in post-harvest processing sector of coconut are neglected or have been rather slow with the result that the increased productivity could not be absorbed by the traditional processing sector. Meanwhile, the production of coconut is expected to reach 20,000 million nuts by the end of this century if the present trend continues. Since the inception of the Board, some R & D efforts in the post-harvest processing of coconut could be streamlined and strengthened. But not much has been achieved. Therefore, the development of appropriate processing technologies for the fuller utilization of the major products and by-products of coconut assumes considerable importance in a country like India. Utilisation of coconut water and skimmed coconut milk in various food preparations, in soft drink preparations, coconut shells for the manufacture of activated carbon etc., are some of the fields yet to be developed and popularized in the country. Efforts should be made to create awareness about the various end uses of coconut and its by-product among the farmers of Tumkur district and also required industrial base for such activities should be established and encouraged in the district.

9. Coir, the golden coloured fibre extracted from the coconut husk, can be put to a multiplicity of end uses. Coir industry in India is an important agro-

based cottage industry and produces a wide range of products from coir fibre and coir yarn and helps to earn much needed foreign exchange to the country. Therefore agro-based cottage industrial units should be established and encouraged by providing technical know-how and finance to the local people in the district so that coconut and its products will be used for various end uses. This also creates a lot of employment to the rural mass.

10. In Karnataka, the processing at the primary level in restricted to the conversion of coconut into ball copra. In the absence of grower's organizations at the primary level to under take processing activities, the farmers are compelled to dispose of the harvested produce every time to the local middleman processors to whom the farmers are invariably indebted. As such, there is no vertical integration in the coconut processing sector in the Tumkur district with the result that the farmers are often deprived of the benefits of price support measures with copra as the base. Hence there is a need to establish grower's organizations at the primary level to undertake processing activities and to create vertical integration in the coconut processing sector in the district. Such organizations will also help the farmers in providing necessary farm inputs and transfer of technology.

BIBLIOGRAPHY

Part - I : Journals and Periodicals

Chandan Mukherjee: Optimal strategy for replantation of coconut trees in Kerala, Centre for Development Studies, Uller, Trivendrum, India, 1975, pp. 10 - 1127.

Chatterjee, R.K. and Ghose, S: A study of tender nut market of Calcutta *Indian Coconut Journal*, Vol. 21, No. 7 & 8, 1990, pp. 18 - 21.

Chikkasubbanna, V. Jayaprasad, K.V. Subiah Thilak and Poonesh, N.M. Effects of maturity on the chemical composition of tender coconut. (Cocosncifera L. Var Arsikere Tale) Water, *Indian Coconut Journal*, 1990, Vol. 20, No. 12, pp. 10 - 13.

Crawford, M.: Coconut poonac as a food for livestock, Trop. Agric. Mag. Ceylon, Agric. Sco., 1940, Vol.44, No.1, p 168.

Dalvi, H.I. and Others: Price spread in the marketing of coconuts in Konkan region of Maharashtra State, *Journal of Plantation Crops*, Vol. 15, No.1, p 198.

Das, P.K.: Movement of whole sale prior of coconuts copra and coconut oil in Kerala during the last two half decades, *Journal of Plantation Crops*, Vol.14, No.2, 1986, pp. 105 - 114.

Das, P.K. : Estimating production costs and returns for coconut in Kerala, *Journal of Plantation Crops*, Vol.12, No.2, 1994.

George, M.V. and Joseph, P.T : A scheme for stabilization of coconut prices in Kerala, Southern Economist, Vol.12, No.16, 1973.

George, M.V., Thommen, K.J. and Sukurmarna, A.S.: *Incidence of Root (Wilt) and Leaf-rot Diseased and Oryetes infestation symposium plantation crops* (Ed) Venkataraman C.S., pp. 27 - 28.

George, M.V., K.V. Vijayakumar and Jacob Mathew Trend in area production and productivity of coconut in India, Indian Coconut Journal, 1991, Vol. XXII, Nos. 6 & 7, oo 45 - 48.

Gita Aravamutham: Stunted coconut Economy, *Economics and Politically Weekly*, Vol.13, No.19, 1978.

Gopalan: The coconut palm, *Indian Coconut Journal*, Vol.7, No.8, 1954, pp. 15 - 52.

————————, : Improvement of the coconut crop by selection, *Malya Agricultural Journal*, Vol. 20, No.18, 1951, pp. 30 - 39.

Hanz Kaunitz and Conrado S. Daynt: Coconut oil consumption and coronary heart disease, *Journal of Plantation Crops*, Vol. XXV, No.8, 1994, pp. 13 - 15.

Herath, H.M.G.: Economics of the holdings development approach in coconut - Some Preliminary Results, *Journal of Plantation Crops*, Vol. 26.

Jakhade, V.M. and Kurian, A.P. : Credit needs of manuring coconut palms in Kerala, *R.B.I. Bulletin*, Vol. 23, No.9, 1969, pp. 1414 - 27.

Jamool Unni: Changes in the cropping pattern in Kerala, Some evidences on substitution of coconut for Rice, 1960-61 to 1978-79, *Economics and Political Weekly*, Vol.6, No.2, 1973, pp. 252 - 69.

Jose Abraham: T.S.S. Rawther, P.M. Jacob and Robert Cecil: Trend in yield of root affected coconut palm, *Journal of Plantation Crops*, Vol.15, No.6, 1984, pp. 38 - 43.

Krishaji, N. and Chandan Mukherjee and Others: Cropping in the coconut gardens of Kerala, Some preliminary results, *Journal of Plantation Crops*, Vol. 12, No.8, 1976, pp. 1 - 25.

Kuni Krishnan: Coconut the tree of health, *Yojana*, Vol.21, No.6, 1977, pp. 2 - 20.

Kurup, P.A. and Rajmohan, T.: Consumption of coconut oil and coconut kernel and incidence of Atherosclerosis, *Indian Journal of Coconut*, Vol. XXV, No.3, 1994, pp. 2 - 16.

Latha Bastine, C.: Cost and returns in different sizes of coconut holdings in Northern Kerala, India, *Journal of Plantation Crops*, Vol. 18, No.4, 1984, pp. 369 - 372.

Madappa, P.P.: A Study of cost of production of coffee in India, *Indian Journal of Agriculture*, Vol. 25, No.4, 1967, pp. 16 - 26.

Mathew, C.: Summar irrigation to coconut palms, Coconut Bulletin, Indian, N.S., Vol.5, No.12, 1972, pp. 2 -3.

M. Meerabai, B.K. Jayachandran, M., Abdul Salam and Kunjamma, P., Mathew: Cooking Fuel productivity of Coconut trees, Indian Coconut Journal, Vol. XXII, No.8, 1991, pp. 13 - 14.

Nagaraj, N., Shastri, K.N.R. and Chandrakanth : Economic considerations in selecting coconut enterprise. Department of Agricultural Sciences, Bangalore, Indian Journal of Plantation Crops, Vol.15, No.1, 1987, pp. 15 - 22.

Prafulla K. Das: Price behaviour of coconut oil in relation to major oils in India, *Journal of Plantation Crops*, Vol. 18, No.2, 1991, pp. 376 - 382.

Punnathara, C.J.: Cost of Production of Wheat in Punjab during the 1973 - 74 crop season, Punjab Agricultural University, Ludhiana, *Agricultural Situation in India*, Vol. 12, No.6, 1975, pp. 441 - 443.

Raman, M.H. and Kashem, M.A.: Growing and marketing problems of pulse crops in Bangla Desh, Economic Affairs. Vol. 11, No.8, 1993, pp. 24 - 30.

Shastri, K.N.R.M.G., Chandrakanth, R., Nagaraj: Economic considerations in selecting coconut enterprise, Journal of Plantation Crops, Vol. 15, No.1, 1987, pp. 15 - 22.

Vishwanathan, Pillai's: Coconut versatile crop of Kerala, Southern Economists, Vol.14, No.14, 1975, pp. 24 - 25.

Part - II : Books and Reports

Belfort, R. and Hoyer, A.J.: *All about Coconut*, London, St., Catherine Press, 1914, pp. 1 - 36.

Brain, E.: Grim Wood: *Coconut palm products*, Institute London, Food and Agriculture Organisation of the United Nations, 1975, pp. 10 - 120.

Central Plantation Crops Research Institute: Coconut Root (Wilt) Disease: A survey report, CPCRI, Kasargod, 1985, p 15.

Chandan Mukherjee : Optimal strategy for replantation of coconut trees in Kerala, Centre for Development Studies, Uller, Trivendrum, India, 1975, pp. 10 - 112.

Child, R.: *Coconuts*, Longman Group Ltd., London, 1974, pp. 2 - 42.

Coconut Planters Manual: *Ferguson's all about the coconut palm*. Colombo, Ceylon, Observer Press, 1923, pp. 1 - 120.

Copeiand, E.B.: *The coconut*, MacMillan and Co. Ltd., London, 1937, pp. 5 - 20.

John, M.C.: *Coconut cultivation*, ICAR Publishers, New Delhi, 1970, pp. 1 - 50.

Mandal, R.C.: *Coconut production and protection Technology*, Agro Botanical Publishers, India, 1991, pp. 1 - 155.

Menon, K.P.V. and Pandalai, K.M.: The coconut palm - A monograph, Indian Central Coconut Committee, Ernakulam, 1960, pp. 20 - 50.

Markose, V.T.: Coconut development in India, Coconut Development Board, Bangalore, 1980, pp. 701 - 707.

Narasimhappa, C.: *Processing and Marketing of coconut and its products*, Processing and Marketing of coconuts in India,

Coconut Development Board, Ministry of Agriculture, Govt. of India, Cochin, Kerala, India, 1987, pp. 129 - 132.

Narayan and others: *Coconut Development in Kerala, Expert evaluation,* Centre for Development Studies, Trivendrum, 1991, pp. 1 - 56.

Patel J.S.: *The Coconut - a monograph* - Govt. Press, Madras 1938, pp. 8 - 26.

Pathiyagoda, V.: *Hand book on Coconut Cultivation,* Coconut Research Institute of Srilanka, Lunwila, 1982, pp. 1 - 5.

Popenoe, J.: *Coconut and Cashew,* North American tree nuts, Geneva, N.Y., W.F. Humphrey Press, 1969, pp.. 2 - 115.

Raveendra, O.: Demand consumption pattern and consumer Acceptibility of Desiccated Coconut, Coconut Development Board, Ministry of Agriculture, Govt. of India, Cochin, Kerala, India, 1987, pp. 120 - 124.

Rebello, N.S.P., Chengappa, P.G. and Lalitha Achoth: *An Analysis of Arrivals and prices of coconuts in principal coconut markets in Karnataka,* Coconut Development Board, Ministry of Agriculture, Govt. of India, Cochin, Kerala, India, 1987, pp. 142 - 143.

Sampson, H.C.: *The Coconut palm,* Jone Balesons nd Daniels Son Ltd., London, 1923, pp. 1 - 622.

Thampan, P.K.: *Promoting product diversification and by products utilization in Coconut Industry in India,* Coconut Development Board, Ministry of Agriculture, Govt. of India, Cochin, Kerala, India, pp. 33 - 42.

————: *Glimpses of coconut industry in India,* Edited by Muhammed Edchal and T.B. Nandakumar. Coconut Development Board, Cochin, 1988, p 219.

————: Hand book of Coconut Palm, Oxford and IBH Pub. Co., New Delhi, 1981, pp. 4 - 126.

————: Portable Coconut Growing, Coconut Development Board, Ministry of Agriculture, Govt. of India, Cochin, Kerala, 1984, pp. 4 - 56.

Government of India, Sixth Five Year Plan, Statisticals, Outlays and Programmes 1980-85, Planning Department. Vol. I, Bangalore.

Government of Karnataka, Draft Seventh Five Year Plan, 1985 - 1990. Planning Department, Bangalore.

————: Eighth Five Year Plan, (1992 - 1997), Vol.1, Planning Department, Bangalore.

————: Karnataka at a Glance, 1991-1992, Directorate of Economics and Statistics, Bangalore, 1992.

————: Tumkur District At a Glance, 1994-1995, District Statistical Office, Tumkur, 1985.